HEN

WHAT THE
OLD
TESTAMENT
IS ALL ABOUT

G/L
REGAL
BOOKS

A Division of G/L Publications
Glendale, California, U.S.A.

©Copyright 1977 by G/L Publications
All rights reserved

Published by
Regal Books Division, G/L Publications
Glendale, California 91209
Printed in U.S.A.

Library of Congress Catalog Card No. 76-51196
ISBN 0-8307-0466-3

The Scripture quotations are from the *New American Standard Bible.* ©The Lockman Foundation 1960, 1962, 1963, 1968, 1971. Used by permission.

Contents

A teaching manual and discussion guide for use with
this book are available from your church supplier.

Abbreviations of Books of the Bible

Acts	Acts	Kings	Kings
Amos	Amos	Lamentations	Lam.
Chronicles	Chron.	Leviticus	Lev.
Colossians	Col.	Luke	Luke
Corinthians	Cor.	Malachi	Mal.
Daniel	Dan.	Mark	Mark
Deuteronomy	Deut.	Matthew	Matt.
Ecclesiastes	Eccles.	Micah	Mic.
Ephesians	Eph.	Nahum	Nah.
Esther	Esther	Nehemiah	Neh.
Exodus	Exod.	Numbers	Num.
Ezekiel	Ezek.	Obadiah	Obad.
Ezra	Ezra	Peter	Pet.
Galatians	Gal.	Philemon	Philem.
Genesis	Gen.	Philippians	Phil.
Habakkuk	Hab.	Proverbs	Prov.
Haggai	Hag.	Psalm	Ps.
Hebrews	Heb.	Revelation	Rev.
Hosea	Hos.	Romans	Rom.
Isaiah	Isa.	Ruth	Ruth
James	Jas.	Samuel	Sam.
Jeremiah	Jer.	Song of Solomon	Song of Sol.
Job	Job		
Joel	Joel	Thessalonians	Thess.
John	John	Timothy	Tim.
Jonah	Jon.	Titus	Titus
Joshua	Josh.	Zechariah	Zech.
Jude	Jude	Zephaniah	Zeph.
Judges	Judg.		

The Bible, God's Book

Behind and beneath the Bible, above and beyond the Bible, is the God of the Bible. The Bible is God's written revelation of His will to men. Its central theme is salvation through Jesus Christ.

The word "Bible" comes from the Greek word *biblos* and means books. It contains 66 books, written by 40 authors, covering a period of about 1600 years.

The Old Testament was written mostly in Hebrew (a few passages in Aramaic) and the New Testament was written in the Greek language. Our English Bible is a translation from these original languages.

The authors were kings and princes, poets and philosophers, prophets and statesmen. Some were learned men and others were unschooled fishermen.

OLD TESTAMENT BOOKS

5 Law
12 Historical
5 Poetical

17 Prophetic
(5 Major)
(12 Minor)

NEW TESTAMENT BOOKS

4 Gospels	21 Epistles
1 History	(14 Pauline)
1 Prophecy	(7 General)

The Old Testament begins with God (Gen. 1:1) and the New Testament with Christ. From Adam to Abraham we have the history of the human race and from Abraham to Christ the history of the chosen race. From Christ on we have the history of the Church. In the Old Testament we find the covenant of law. In the New Testament we find the covenant of grace which came through Jesus Christ. One led into the other (Gal. 3:17-25).

"Most people's knowledge of history is like a string of graduated pearls without the string," said an historian. This statement seems to be especially true of Bible history. Many people know the Bible characters and the principal events, but they are hopelessly lost when they are called upon to connect the stories in order. Anyone who has experienced the thrill of learning to place the individual characters in their right setting can realize the difference it makes in his enjoyment of God's Word. Here are some outlines to help you place people and events in order.

OLD TESTAMENT PRINCIPAL CHARACTERS

1. God	7. Jacob
2. Satan	8. Joseph
3. Adam	9. Pharaoh
4. Noah	10. Moses
5. Abraham	11. Aaron
6. Isaac	12. Caleb

13. Joshua
14. Othniel ⎤
15. Deborah ⎟
16. Barak ⎟ 15
17. Gideon ⎬ Judges
18. Jephthah ⎟
19. Samson ⎦
20. Ruth
21. Samuel
22. Saul
23. David
24. Solomon
25. Elijah
26. Elisha

27. Kings of Israel (19)
28. Jehoshaphat ⎤
29. Hezekiah ⎬ 20 Kings
30. Josiah ⎦ of Judah
31. Isaiah ⎤
32. Jeremiah ⎟
33. Ezekiel ⎬ Prophets
34. Daniel ⎦
35. Nebuchadnezzar
36. Cyrus
37. Zerubbabel
38. Ezra
39. Nehemiah
40. Esther

NEW TESTAMENT PRINCIPAL CHARACTERS
1. John the Baptist
2. Christ
3-14. Disciples (12)
15. Stephen
16. Philip
17. Paul
18. James, brother of Jesus

PRINCIPAL PERIODS
I. Period of the Patriarchs to Moses—Genesis
   A. The godly line—leading events:
      1. Creation
      2. Fall
      3. Flood
      4. Dispersion
   B. The chosen family—leading events:
      1. Call of Abraham
      2. The descent into Egypt—bondage
II. Period of Great Leaders: Moses to Saul—Exodus to Samuel

A. Exodus from Egypt
B. Wandering in wilderness
C. Conquest of Canaan
D. Rule of the Judges

III. Period of the Kings: Saul to the Captivities—
Samuel, Kings, Chronicles, the Prophetic Books
A. The United Kingdom
1. Saul
2. David
3. Solomon
B. The Divided Kingdom
1. Judah
2. Israel

IV. Period of Foreign Rulers:
Captivities to Christ—
Ezra, Nehemiah, Esther, Daniel and Ezekiel
A. Captivity of Israel
B. Captivity of Judah
C. Restoration of Judah

V. Christ—the Gospels

VI. The Church—Acts and the Epistles
A. In Jerusalem
B. Extending to the Gentiles
C. In all the world

GOD'S LIVING WORD

Remember that in God's Word the foundation of Christianity is laid in the revelation of the one and only true God. The Bible tells us of the origin of sin and how it separated man from God. Then we find the promise of a Saviour, One who was to come *to seek and to save that which was lost . . . and to give*

9

His life a ransom for many (Luke 19:10; Matt. 20: 28). We see all through the ages one purpose is evident; the coming of the Redeemer of the world who would save those who believe in Him from sin.

There is no royal road to learning and certainly there is no royal road to knowledge of the Bible. The Spirit of God will lead us into all truth, to be sure, but God's command is that we study to be approved, workmen unashamed (see 2 Tim. 2:15).

Do you want to read the Bible through? Leave 80 hours for it. Plot out that time. How much time can you give each day? How many days a week? If we are going to know the Bible, we must adjust our lives to make time. Otherwise we shall never come into a worthy knowledge of the Word; for it is impossible to get from others that personal knowledge of the Word which is possible and is indeed needful.

The Bible is both divine and human. The thought is divine, the revelation is divine, the expression of the communication is human. *Men* (human element) *moved by the Holy Spirit* (divine element) *spoke from God* (see 2 Pet. 1:21).

So we have here a book unlike all others. This divine revelation of God to man communicated through men, moves smoothly from its beginnings to its great end. Bible history takes us into the unknown past and its prophecies take us into the otherwise unknown future. The Old Testament is the foundation; the New Testament is the superstructure. A foundation is of no value unless a building is built upon it. A building is impossible without a foundation. So the Old Testament and New Testament are essential to one another.

10

INTERESTING FACTS ABOUT THE BIBLE

Christ quotes from 22 Old Testament books. In Matthew there are 19 Old Testament quotations; in Mark 15; in Luke 25; in John 11; in Hebrews 85 (quotations and allusions); in Revelation 245.

Number of verses—31,102

Longest chapter—Psalm 119

Shortest chapter—Psalm 117

Longest verse—Esther 8:9

Shortest verse—John 11:35

Longest book in Old Testament—Psalms

Longest book in New Testament—Luke

CHRIST, THE LIVING WORD

The Old Testament is an account of a nation (the Hebrew nation). The New Testament is an account of a Man (the Son of man). The nation was founded and nurtured of God to bring the Man into the world.

God Himself became a man so that we might know what to think of when we think of God (John 1:14; 14:9). His appearance on the earth is the central event of all history. The Old Testament sets the stage for it. The New Testament describes it.

As a man Christ lived the most perfect life ever known. He was kind, tender, gentle, patient and sympathetic. He loved people. He worked marvelous miracles to feed the hungry. The weary, pain-ridden and heartsick came to Him and He gave them rest. If all the deeds of kindness that He did were written, the world would not contain the books (John 21:25).

Then He died—to take away the sin of the world, and to become the Saviour of men. He rose from the dead and is alive today. He is not merely an historical

11

character, but a living Person—the most important fact of history, and the most vital force in the world today. And He promises eternal life to all who come to Him. The whole Bible is built around the story of Christ and His promise of life everlasting to men. It was written that we might believe, understand, know, love and follow Him.

THE BIBLE, GOD'S WRITTEN WORD

Apart from any theory of inspiration, any theory of how the Bible books came to their present form, how much the text may have suffered in passing through the hands of editors and copyists; or what is historical and what may be poetical, assume that the Bible is just what it appears to be. Accept the books as we have them in our Bible. Study them to know their contents. You will find there is a unity of thought which indicates that One Mind inspired the writing of the whole series of books; that it bears on its face the stamp of its Author; that it is in every sense the WORD OF GOD.

Minimum Daily Requirements/Spiritual Vitamins
Sunday: God-given (2 Tim. 3:10-17)
Monday: Should be treasured (Deut. 11:1-9; Josh. 1:8,9)
Tuesday: Should be kept (Ps. 119:9-18)
Wednesday: A lamp (Ps. 119:105-117)
Thursday: Food (Isa. 55:1-11; Matt. 4:4)
Friday: Fulfilled (Luke 24:36-45)
Saturday: Complete (Rev. 22:8-21)

Genesis, Book of Beginnings

Genesis is the seed-plot of the Word of God. The title Genesis, which is Greek, means origin, and the first word in the Hebrew of Genesis is translated "in the beginning"—words which indicate both the scope and the limits of the book. It tells us the beginning of everything except God. Upon its truths all the future revelation of God to man is built up.

GENESIS IS THE BOOK OF BEGINNINGS
1. The beginning of the world (Gen. 1:1-25)
2. The beginning of the human race (1:26—2:25)
3. The beginning of sin in the world (3:1-7)
4. The beginning promise of redemption (3:8-24)
5. The beginning of family life (4:1-15)
6. The beginning of man-made civilization (4:16—9:29)
7. The beginning of nations (chaps. 10,11)
8. The beginning of the Hebrew race (chaps. 12—50)

Genesis records the beginnings of all these things.

No wonder that when men, because of spiritual blindness (Eph. 4:18), reject God's revelation in this peerless record of beginnings, they worship chance as the creator, beasts as their ancestors, and fallen humanity as the flower of natural evolution!

Genesis records at least 2000 years of history. However, it is a spiritual interpretation of history. In two chapters God flashes on the wall an account of the creation of the world and of man. From there on we see God bringing lost man back to Himself.

Satan attacks this majestic book. Its authorship by Moses, its scientific accuracy, and its literal testimony to human sin as deliberate disobedience to God have all been bitterly assailed. The Word of God, however, definitely declares Genesis to be one of the living oracles delivered to Moses. To its infallible truth and its testimony to the Messiah, our Lord Jesus set His seal (John 5:46,47).

When Genesis goes, a divine Creator, a divine creation, a divinely promised Redeemer, and a divinely inspired Bible must also go. Around its sacred pages is the protection of the Holy Spirit of God who inspired its words.

WHO WROTE GENESIS?

The age-long Hebrew and Christian position is that Moses, guided by the Spirit of God, wrote Genesis. The book closes something like 300 years before Moses was born. Moses could have received his information by direct revelation from God (Amos 3:7) or from historical records handed down from his forefathers to which he had access. Every year archaeologists dig up in Egypt and Palestine evidences

14

of writing in Moses' day and of the historical truth of what is recorded in the Pentateuch. Moses was educated in the palace of Pharaoh (Acts 7:22) and made use of writing (Exod. 34:27; Num. 17:2; Deut. 6:9; 24:1,3). See what Jesus said about Moses in Luke 24:27 and John 7:19.

WHO WROTE THE CREATION STORY USED BY MOSES?

No doubt it was written long before, maybe by Abraham or Noah or Enoch. Who knows? Writing was in common use before the days of Abraham. In Ur, as in every important city in Babylon, there were libraries with thousands of books, dictionaries, grammars, reference works, encyclopedias, and works on mathematics, astronomy, geography, religion and politics. No doubt Abraham received traditions or records from Shem about the story of creation, the fall of man, and the flood. He no doubt made careful and accurate records of all that happened to him and of the promises God made to him. He put it down on clay tablets in the cuneiform writing to be handed down in the annals of the nation he was founding.

CREATION Genesis 1,2

As the Book of Genesis begins we see these words untarnished by the ages, *In the beginning God created the heavens and the earth.* In these few words we have the Bible declaration of the origin of this material universe. God called all things into being by the word of His power. He spoke and worlds were framed (Heb. 11:3). Interpretations of the method of God may vary but the truth of the fact remains.

15

God's creative work was progressive:
1. The world of matter (Gen. 1:3-19)
2. The system of life (Gen. 1:20-25)
3. Man, the crown of creation (Gen. 1:26,27)

Who was the God mentioned so many times in the first 31 verses of Genesis? Read John 1:1 and Hebrews 1:1. Here we see that the One who redeemed us by His precious blood, our Saviour, was the Creator of this universe. Someone has said that God the Father is the architect; God the Son, the builder; and God the Holy Spirit, the beautifier of the universe. We find the Holy Spirit in Genesis 1:2.

In chapter 1 we have the account of creation in outline, in chapter 2 part of the same in detail. The detail concerns the creation of man, for the Bible is the history of the redemption of man.

Know this, God created man in His own image to have fellowship with Himself. Man cut himself off from God by sin. It is only when sin is removed that we can have fellowship again. This is why Jesus Christ came to this earth (1 Pet. 2:24). Read in 1 John chapter 1 how sin keeps us not only from fellowship with God but with one another. First John 1:9 tells us what we can do to have a restored fellowship.

THE FALL Genesis 3,4

Adam and Eve were created in a state of innocence but with the power of choice. They were tested under the most favorable circumstances. They were endowed with clear minds and pure hearts, with the ability to do right. God gave them His own presence and fellowship (Gen. 3:8).

Satan, the author of sin, acting through a serpent,

tempted them to doubt God's Word. They yielded to the temptation and failed in the test. Here sin entered the world. Satan still influences men to disobey God. The results of Adam and Eve's sin are enumerated in Genesis 3. They were separated from God, the ground was cursed, and sorrow filled their hearts.

In mercy God promised One who would redeem men from sin (Gen. 3:15). The seed of the woman (the virgin-born Jesus) would come to destroy the works of the devil (1 John 3:8).

Immediately after "the fall" men began to offer sacrifices unto the Lord. No doubt these sacrifices were ordered of God. They kept before man the fact of his fall and of the coming sacrifice. It would be by the shedding of this blood that he was to be redeemed from sin and death (Heb. 9:22).

Long before God gave the law to Moses (Exod. 20), we find several ordinances given in Genesis. At the very beginning God instituted the Sabbath (Gen. 2:1-3) and marriage (Gen. 2:24). The tithe was evidently observed. Read Abraham's words in Genesis 14:20 and Jacob's words in Genesis 28:22. God has evidently made man realize from the very beginning that he was only a steward of all that he had.

THE FIRST CIVILIZATION

The civilization before the flood is called the antediluvian civilization. It was the civilization started by Cain. It ended in destruction and perished in the flood. The Bible teaches and the archaeologist confirms that the people of the world before the flood were not mere savages. They had attained a considerable degree of civilization. Some of their actual places of abode have been discovered and some relics of their handwork which have been uncovered give evidence of a civilization such as the Bible seems to describe in Genesis 4:16-22.

In cities, such as Ur, or Ubaid, the layer of silt left by the flood has been found by Professor Woolley, an archaeologist sent out by the British Museum and Pennsylvania University. Underneath the flood deposit of Ur layers of rubbish full of stone and flint instruments, colored pottery, seals and burnt brick were found. The same is true of other cities.

THE FLOOD Genesis 5—9

The account of the flood in the Bible is very plain and straightforward. After the fall God gave the world a new beginning but soon the wickedness of man increased until there remained only one righteous man, Noah. Evil had grown rampant and threatened to destroy everything that was good. Adam and Eve yielded to an outward temptation, but now man yielded to temptation within (Gen. 6:5).

God had been long-suffering in His patience with men. The Holy Spirit had striven with men. Noah had warned them for 120 years while he was building the ark. Even after Noah and his wife and his three sons and their wives, taking with them two of every unclean animal and fourteen of every clean animal, had entered into the ark of safety, there was a respite of seven days before the flood came. But God's mercies were refused and so men had to perish (6; 7). Noah was saved from the flood in the ark. When he came out, the first thing he did was to erect an altar and worship God (8:20).

18

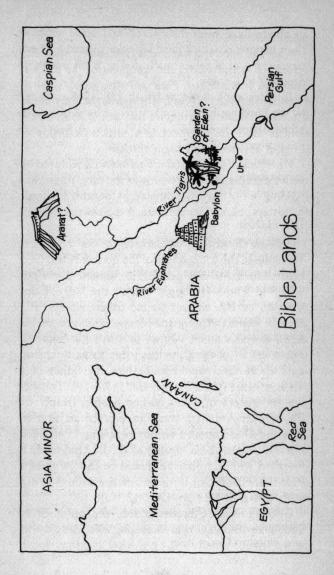

Bible Lands

Caspian Sea

Persian Gulf

Garden of Eden?

River Tigris

Ararat?

River Euphrates

Babylon

Ur

ARABIA

ASIA MINOR

CANAAN

Mediterranean Sea

Red Sea

EGYPT

BABEL Genesis 10,11

After the flood the world was given a new start. But instead of spreading out and repopulating the earth as God had commanded, men built the great tower of Babel in defiance of God. They thought they could establish a worldwide empire that would be independent of God. In judgment God sent a confusion of tongues and scattered them abroad.

The cities of this period are rather well pictured by the archaeologists. The tower was the most important building in the town. Scientists feel that this fondness for towers reached its ultimate in the tower of Babel.

THE CALL OF ABRAHAM Genesis 12—38

In spite of the wickedness of the human heart, God wanted to show His grace. He wanted a chosen people to whom He might entrust the Holy Scriptures; to be His witness to the other nations; and through whom the promised Messiah could come. He called a man named Abram to leave his home in idolatrous Ur of the Chaldees to go to an unknown land where God would make him the father of a mighty nation (Gen. 12:1-3; Heb. 11:8-19). This begins the history of God's chosen people, Israel.

Wherever Abraham went, he erected an altar to God and God honored him by revealing Himself to him. He was called a "friend of God." God made a covenant with him that he should be the father of a great nation and that through him the nations of the earth would be blessed (Gen. 12:1-3).

Through Isaac, Abraham's son, the promises of God were passed down to Jacob, who, despite his many faults, valued God's covenant blessing. Jacob in his wanderings suffered for his sin, and through chastening came out a great man. His name was changed to Israel (32:28). This is the name by which God's chosen people were called—Israelites. Ten of Jacob's twelve sons and two of his grandsons by Joseph became the heads of the 12 tribes of Israel. Read Genesis 49.

DESCENT INTO EGYPT Genesis 39—50

Isaac and Rebecca made the mistake of playing favorites with their two sons. Isaac favored the hunter Esau. Rebecca favored the quiet Jacob. Jacob did the same thing with his son Joseph. This favoritism aroused jealousy in the other sons. Joseph is one of the outstanding noble characters of the Old Testament. It was through Joseph that Jacob's family was transplanted into Egypt. Joseph's life is one of the most perfect illustrations in the Bible of God's overruling providence. He was sold as a slave at 17. At 30 he became ruler in Egypt; 10 years later his father, Jacob, entered Egypt.

Jacob and his sons and their children, numbering 70 in all, went down into Egypt because of a famine in Canaan. There they were exalted by the Pharaoh who was reigning at that time. When he learned that they were shepherds, he permitted them to settle in the land of Goshen where they grew in number, wealth and influence under the "shepherd kings of Egypt."

Read Jacob's dying words to his 12 sons (Gen. 49). We see here again the promise of Shiloh (Christ) who is to be the coming ruler. Christ is also called the Lion of the tribe of Judah (see Rev. 5:5).

The Book of Genesis ends in failure. The last words are *in a coffin in Egypt.* Only death marks the pathway of sin; *the wages of sin is death* (Rom. 6:23). The people needed a Saviour!

There are eight names mentioned in Genesis that we should remember in order: God, Adam, Satan, Noah, Abraham, Isaac, Jacob, Joseph.

There are six places of supreme importance in connection with the history of Genesis—Eden, Mount Ararat, Babel, Ur of the Chaldees, Canaan (Promised Land), Egypt.

Minimum Daily Requirements/Spiritual Vitamins
Sunday: Creation (Gen. 1:1-5,26-31; 2:7-22)
Monday: Fall (Gen. 3:1-24)
Tuesday: Deluge (Gen. 6:1-7; 7:7-24; 8:6-11,18-22; 9:1-16)
Wednesday: Beginnings of languages (Gen. 11:1-9)
Thursday: The Abrahamic call and covenant (Gen. 12:1-9; 13:14-18; 15:1-21; 17:4-8; 22:15-20; 26:1-5; 28:10-15)
Friday: Story of Joseph (Gen. 37:1-36; 42)
Saturday: Jacob's final blessing (Gen. 49)

Exodus and God's Redeeming Love

3

Genesis tells of man's failure, but Exodus is the thrilling epic of God's rescuing of man. It tells of the redeeming work of a sovereign God. It begins in darkness and gloom, yet ends in glory; it commences by telling how God came down in grace to deliver an enslaved people, and ends by declaring how God came down in glory to dwell in the midst of a redeemed people. Exodus, which is Greek, means "way out."

SOME THINGS TO REMEMBER IN EXODUS

The Great Hero, Moses

The book gives the story of Moses, the great hero of God. Moody said that Moses spent 40 years thinking he was somebody; 40 years learning he was nobody, and 40 years discovering what God can do with a nobody. Read Hebrews 11:23-29.

23

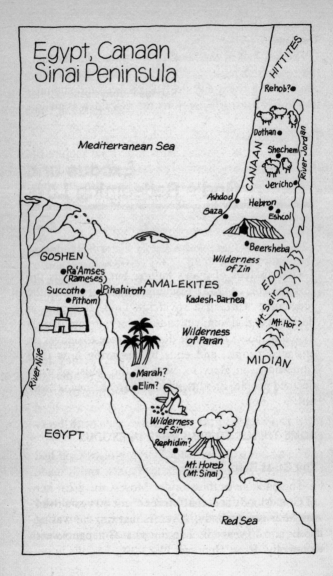

Egypt, Canaan
Sinai Peninsula

HITTITES

Rehob?

Mediterranean Sea

CANAAN

Dothan

Shechem

River Jordan

Jericho

Ashdod

Hebron

Gaza

Eshcol

Beersheba

GOSHEN

Ra'Amses
(Rameses)

Wilderness
of Zin

Succoth

Pihahiroth

AMALEKITES

Pithom

Kadesh-Barnea

EDOM

Mt. Seir

Mt. Hor?

Wilderness
of Paran

MIDIAN

River Nile

Marah?

Elim?

EGYPT

Wilderness
of Sin

Rephidim?

Mt. Horeb
(Mt. Sinai)

Red Sea

The Law

The last half of the book (19—40) teaches us that the redeemed must do the will of their Redeemer, consecrating themselves to His service, and submitting to His control. Therefore, the moral law is given.

The Tabernacle

God gave the Tabernacle as a detailed picture of the Redeemer to come in His many offices and as a dwelling place for His visible glory on earth. Its wonderful typology is rich in Christian truth.

THE BONDAGE Exodus 1—11

The Book of Genesis is a family history. Exodus is a national history. As Exodus opens—three and a half centuries have passed since the closing scene of Genesis. When Joseph died and a new dynasty came to the throne in Egypt, the wealth and great numbers of the Israelites made them objects of suspicion in the eyes of the Egyptians. (There were only 70 persons who went down into Egypt, but before they left Egypt the people had grown into a nation of approximately 3,000,000.) The Pharaohs, wishing to break with them, reduced them to slavery. This was hard for a people who had lived as free men with every favor.

The Israelites remembered the promises God had given to Abraham and his descendants, and it made bondage doubly hard to understand (Gen. 12:1-3).

The story of Exodus is repeated in every soul who seeks deliverance from the enmeshing and enervating influence of the world. The things that happen were written for our admonition. We study Exodus in order to see God's way of delivering sinful man, and His gracious purposes in thus rescuing him.

THE PASSOVER Exodus 12—19

Exodus 12 gives us the thrilling story of the Passover, the clearest Old Testament picture of our individual salvation through faith in the shed blood of our Lord Jesus Christ. In this chapter is the basis for calling Christ the Lamb of God and the many tender references to His crucifixion as the death of our own Passover Lamb (1 Cor. 5:7).

Perhaps the children of Israel did not know the significance of this feast the night before they left Egypt, but they believed God and obeyed.

God had sent nine plagues on Egypt in order to make Pharaoh willing to let His people go. Almost a year had passed and with each plague there was a hardening of Pharaoh's heart. Finally God said that the firstborn in all Egypt should die. It would have fallen on the Hebrews, too, had they not killed the paschal lamb and been protected by its blood of redemption (Exod. 12:12,13). Every person should study the divine order of the Passover in Exodus 12.

1. Take a Lamb

It was not the spotlessness of the living lamb that saved them (Heb. 9:22; 1 John 1:7; Rev. 1:5). It was not Christ's sinless life that saves us, but His death on the cross. Read Hebrews 9:28; Isaiah 53:6; John 19:14; 1 Corinthians 5:7.

2. Sprinkle the Blood

It is not enough for the lamb to be slain. Every

Israelite individually had to apply it to his own household (Exod. 12:22). The blood on the lintel is what saved them. It was not what they thought about it, but what they did with it that counted. *When I see the blood I will pass over you* (Exod. 12:13). Not all the blood shed on Calvary's cross can save a soul from death unless it is applied, then—*When I see the blood I will pass over you.* Read Hebrews 9:22.

3. Eat the Lamb

After the blood was shed and sprinkled, then there was direction for nourishment, etc. So with us. Salvation first, then feeding—fellowship, worship, walk and service. Feeding did not save them, but blood first; then nourishment was possible.

The lamb was to be feasted upon not raw, not unbaked, but a suffering lamb who passed through fire. Nothing was to be left—eaten in haste and nothing remaining. Not a bone broken! Christ's body was broken but not His bones (Ps. 34:20; John 19:36).

4. Remove the Leaven

Leaven of unrighteousness must be removed from our lives if we are to eat with God.

5. Bitter Herbs

Christ tasted the bitter cup for us and we too must suffer (Heb. 12:11).

6. Be Ready to Leave

They ate standing—not knowing how soon they would go, all provisions made for the journey. What a contrast that night—peaceful feasting in the houses of Israel; awful mourning in the houses of Egypt!

We have read here of the Passover. Then came the Passage. The Passover sealed them; the Passage of the Red Sea steeled them. They left Egypt under the blood, marked men; they passed through the Red Sea directed, determined men.

Up to this time in Israel's history all had been grace and mercy. God had heard the cry of their bondage and answered them. God selected a leader and trained him. God defeated their enemies. God fed them. And yet they rebelled. Then a new order of things was brought about at Sinai.

THE GIVING OF THE LAW Exodus 20—24

In Exodus 20—24 the law was given, broken and restored. The law demanded nothing short of perfection (see Ps. 19:7-11). Only one Man has been able to keep it perfectly. Christ not only kept the law but He paid the complete penalty for the broken law. Christ suffered that we might be spared (see Heb. 9:13-15; 10:1-22; 1 Pet. 1:18-20).

If man could not keep the law, why was it given? That we might know our exceeding sinfulness. The law did not make man sin, but it showed him that he was a sinner (read Gal. 3:24; Rom. 7:12; 8:1-4; 3:19-28). The physician comes and looks at a child and the symptoms reveal that he has measles. He gives him some medicine that makes him break out. The doctor did not make the child have measles, but he proved that measles was there.

There are two mountain peaks which stand over against each other in God's Word. Mount Sinai with all of its horror thundered forth the law (Exod. 19).

Opposite this God places Calvary. Calvary took away all the fire and thunder and made possible a meeting place between God and the sinner. We each have a choice as to how we shall approach God, either by law or by blood (Heb. 12:18-29).

Laws may be divided into two parts: laws regarding man's attitude toward God and laws regarding man's attitude toward his fellowman. God gave the whole testimony (Exod. 20:1) and man assumed the responsibility of keeping it (read Exod. 19:8).

THE BUILDING OF THE TABERNACLE
Exodus 25—40

Exodus 25—40 gives us one of the richest veins in inspiration's exhaustless mines. We must use our imagination and reason as we enter the holy precincts and gaze upon the significant furniture. God told Moses He wished a sanctuary or holy dwelling place. It pointed to Christ and told of His person and work.

The Outer Court

Here we see the brazen altar on which the burnt offerings were sacrificed (27:1-8). Remember, Christ is our burnt offering. The laver was there for the cleansing of the priests before they could enter into the holy place to render their service (30:18).

The Holy Place

Herein was the golden candlestick (25:31-40), typifying Christ, the Light of the world; and the table of shewbread (25:23-30), for Christ who is the Bread of life; and the golden altar of incense (30:1-10), symbolizing Christ's intercession for us.

Holy of Holies

Now if we draw back the veil (which typifies the body of Christ), we will see the Ark of the Covenant, the symbol of God's presence. Into this holy of holies the high priest came once a year to sprinkle the blood of atonement. Hebrews tells us that Christ is not only our High Priest but that He was our atonement, and so we can go into the holy of holies (the presence of God) at any time with boldness.

The Tabernacle Itself

The Tabernacle, with the cloud of glory over it, taught the people that God was dwelling in their midst (Exod. 25:8). Critics say that the account of the Tabernacle and its wonderful structure could not be true. They say that the times were too primitive, but research has given abundant evidence of great skill in such matter long before the Exodus. Fine linen was used in many ways. Fine work in gold has been discovered in the tombs dating back to as early as the twelfth Egyptian dynasty, and Moses lived in the eighteenth dynasty.

Minimum Daily Requirements/Spiritual Vitamins
Sunday: Bondage (Exod. 1:1-22)
Monday: The call of Moses (Exod. 3—4)
Tuesday: The Plagues (Exod. 7:20—11:10)
Wednesday: The Passover (Exod. 12:1-51)
Thursday: The Law (Exod. 20:1-26)
Friday: The worship (Exod. 25:1-9; 28:1-14, 30-43)
Saturday: Recommissioned (Exod. 33:12—34:17)

Guidelines for Worship in Leviticus

"Get right," say the offerings. There are five of them: burnt offering, meal offering, peace offering, sin offering, trespass offering.

"Keep right," say the feasts. There are eight of them: Sabbath, Passover, Pentecost, Trumpets, Atonement, Tabernacles, the Sabbath Year and Jubilee.

The Book of Leviticus is God's picture-book for the children of Israel to help them in their religious training. Every picture pointed forward to the work of Jesus Christ.

The title of Leviticus suggests the subject matter—the Levites and the priests and their service in the Tabernacle. It is also called the Book of Laws.

Leviticus is called the Book of Atonement (Lev. 16:30-34). In it God says, *Be holy for I am holy* (Lev. 11:44,45; 19:2; 20:7,26). This book is a timely book for it insists on keeping the body holy as well as the soul. It teaches that the redeemed ones must be holy because their Redeemer is holy. It gives us not only the key for our spiritual life and its holy walk, but it surprises us with real lessons in hygiene and sanitation for the care of the body.

THE FIVE OFFERINGS

One of the most important questions in life is "How may an unholy person approach a holy God?" At the very beginning of the book God makes provision for His people to approach Him in worship. This book shows redeemed Israel that the way to God is by sacrifice.

Isn't it strange that deep down in every heart there is a sense of guilt and the feeling of a need to do something to secure pardon? The pagan brings sacrifices to the altars of his gods, but he cannot see beyond his sacrifice. When we look at the sacrifices in this book, we find that they point to the Perfect Sacrifice for sin which was to be made on Calvary. There can be no fellowship between God and the sinner until sin has been dealt with; the only way is sacrifice (Heb. 9:22).

Learn this simple outline to fix in mind the first six chapters of Leviticus

Burnt Offering—"Surrender" of Christ for the world (Lev. 1).

Meal Offering—"Service" of Christ in life (Lev. 2).

Peace Offering—"Serenity" of Christ in life (Lev. 3).

Sin Offering—"Substitute" of Christ for sin (Lev. 4—5:13).

Trespass Offering—"Satisfaction" by Christ for demands of God (Lev. 5:14—6:7).

Burnt Offering Leviticus 1

The offerings start with the burnt offering and end with the trespass offering. The burnt offering is a type of Christ offering Himself without spot to God. It was an offering of dedication and was the most common of the sacrifices.

Why start with a burnt offering? Because sacrifice comes first. No one begins with God until he has yielded all to God (Lev. 1:3). Dedication is man's part; consecration is God's part. We dedicate ourselves to God; He consecrates us to His service.

Meal Offering Leviticus 2

This is the sacrifice of daily devotion. As the burnt offering typifies Christ in death, so the meal offering typifies Christ in life. The fine flour speaks of the character of Christ—His perfection in thought, in word, in action. We must come to Him first with our whole burnt offering. Then we keep coming with our continual meal offering.

Peace Offering Leviticus 3

This offering represents fellowship and communion with God. It is an offering of thanksgiving. Christ is our peace (Eph. 2:14).

Sin Offering Leviticus 4—5:13

In this offering we see an acknowledgement of sin (Lev. 4:2,3). This offering is for expiation. In the other offerings the offerer comes as a worshiper but he comes here as a convicted sinner. God holds us accountable for our sin. We are like criminals who have been tried, found guilty, and sentenced to death.

33

Trespass Offering Leviticus 5:14—6:7

Christ has even taken care of our sin against others. The blood of the trespass offering cleanses the conscience and sends the trespasser back to the one he has wronged, not only with the principal but with the fifth part added (Lev. 6:5). The injurer is forgiven and the injured becomes an actual gainer.

It is a grave error to suppose you are safe and right if you live up to your own conscience. God has scales. We can never comprehend His holiness. None of these sacrifices forgave sin. They only pointed to the true Sacrifice, God's very own Son.

THE PRIEST Leviticus 8—10

God chose one tribe out of the twelve to care for the Tabernacle—the tribe of Levi. One family of Levites, Aaron's, should be the priests. No man could bring his own sacrifice to God. He must bring it to the priest and he in turn would offer it to God.

The priest went from man to God with the prayers and praises of the people. He stood for them and pleaded their cause. The burdened Israelite who desired to approach God brought his animal to the court of the Tabernacle. At the altar of burnt offerings he laid his hand on the animal's head to express his penitence and consecration. The animal was then killed and its blood sprinkled on the altar.

The priest, representing the worshiper, then came to the laver in which he washed his hands, thus indicating the clean life that should follow the forgiveness of sins. He entered the holy place and came to the altar of incense, where prayer was offered.

THE HIGH PRIEST

One day in the year the high priest passed beyond the veil that separated the holy and the most holy place and stood before the mercy seat, with the blood of the atonement, to intercede for the people.

OUR GREAT HIGH PRIEST

Animal sacrifices are no longer necessary because all sacrifices were fulfilled in Christ. Therefore priests are no longer necessary. Christ is our High Priest (Heb. 2:17; 4:15) and He is at the right hand of the Father making intercession for us. We approach God by Him and Him alone (Heb. 10:12; 7:25; John 14:6). As Sacrifice He establishes the relationship of His people with God. As Priest He maintains that position.

This perfect and eternal priesthood is described in the Book of Hebrews. Heaven, not earth, is the sphere of Christ's priestly ministry. He never appeared in the Temple on earth to offer sacrifice. He went there to preach and teach but not to sacrifice. Except in the sense that all believers are spiritual priests (1 Pet. 2:5), there is no such thing as a priest on earth. It is not necessary that any child of God go before any man on earth to obtain entrance into the presence of God. Every Christian has the right to enter because he knows Jesus Christ (see John 14:6 and Heb. 4:16).

THE EIGHT FEASTS

The first part of Leviticus has to do with offerings and the offerers, the last with feasts and feasters. Eight great festivals are mentioned.

The Feast of the Sabbath Leviticus 23:1-3

The Sabbath was given the foremost place. It was a perpetually recurring feast to be obeyed through the whole year on every seventh day. It was a day of rest, celebrating the finished work of God in creation (Gen. 2:2,3). Most Christians celebrate the first day of the week or the day our Lord arose from the grave (Luke 24:1; Acts 20:7; 1 Cor. 16:2). Thus they celebrate the finished work of redemption.

The Feast of the Passover Leviticus 23:4,5

The Passover spoke of redemption and was celebrated every spring at our Easter time. Every Jew who could, went to Jerusalem. It lasted one day, but the feast of unleavened bread which immediately followed lasted seven days. With these the year commenced. The Jews still celebrated this feast when our Lord was on this earth (Luke 2:41-52; Matt. 26:19; John 13) and they celebrate it today.

The Feast of Pentecost Leviticus 23:15-22

This feast was observed 50 days after the feast of the first fruits (the beginning of Passover). This feast of the first fruits typified Christ's resurrection and ours (1 Cor. 15:20). It was 50 days after Christ's resurrection that the Holy Spirit descended upon the disciples and the Church was born. Pentecost was the birthday of the Church. The death and resurrection of Christ had to be accomplished before the descent of the Holy Spirit.

The Feast of the Trumpets Leviticus 23:23-25

This was the New Year's day of the children of

Israel. It was celebrated in the fall about October.

The Day of Atonement Leviticus 23:26-32

This was the greatest day of the year for God's chosen people. On this day the sins of the nation were confessed. Confession is always the first step toward righteousness. It reveals a right attitude toward sin. It leads to a desire for forgiveness.

On this day all the sins, failures and weaknesses of the people were atoned for. The blood was shed and the sins of the people were covered.

We learn in Leviticus 16 that God was hidden behind a veil in the Tabernacle and man was at a distance (Lev. 16:2). The way was not yet made open for man to approach God. God was shut in from man and man was shut out from God. This was the only day in the year when the high priest was permitted to enter the holy of holies. He went in with an offering for the atonement of the sin of the people. Atonement means "cover." This offering "covered" the sins of the people until the great sacrifice on Calvary was made. None of these offerings "took away" those sins.

The Feast of Tabernacles Leviticus 23:33-36

This was the last feast of the year. It commemorated the time when the Israelites lived in tents during their wilderness journey. It was celebrated in the fall and lasted an entire week. The people lived in booths out-of-doors and heard the reading of the Law.

The Feast of the Passover and the Feast of the Tabernacles kept before the children of Israel the marvelous way in which they were delivered from

Egypt and were sustained in the wilderness. God did not want them to forget the way in which the gods of Egypt were utterly discredited and the great nation of Egypt humbled. These days reminded them of their dependence upon Jehovah and the blessings that would come if they would be obedient to His will.

The Sabbatic Year Leviticus 25

This was the year of meditation and devotion. It was a year-long Sabbath. God impressed the purpose and character of the Sabbath upon the minds of the people by keeping them from any kind of labor for a year. This He did every seven years. God wanted to impress upon them that the very land was holy unto Him. This is why Israel is called the Holy Land.

There was quiet over the whole land during these days. All breathed the spirit of rest and meditation. All industry ceased and the minds of the people were kept on the things of the Lord. The Law was read. There were no debts to worry or mar the spirit of the people during this holy year.

The Year of Jubilee Leviticus 25:8-24

Jubilee was celebrated every fiftieth year. It was inaugurated on the Day of Atonement with the blowing of trumpets. As in the sabbatic year the land was not cultivated. All slaves of Hebrew blood were freed. Jewish writers tell us that the year of Jubilee was observed at the time of the fall of Judah in 586 B.C. References are made to this in Isaiah 5:7-10; 61:1,2; Ezekiel 17:12,13; 46:16-18.

Another outstanding event was that all land was

returned to the family to whom it had been assigned in the original distribution. What a wise provision it was from an economic standpoint. But God no doubt had a more far-reaching plan bearing upon the coming of the Messiah. Every tribal and family register must be carefully kept so that the rights of all would be protected. This would apply to Judah, the tribe from which the Messiah was to come. From these registers our Lord's natural descent would be traced exactly.

The Book of Exodus is the book of redemption, but the Book of Leviticus tells how the redeemed ones can worship God. Only through the blood of Christ can we have access to God. God demands a holiness that Christ alone can give, for "He is our Holiness." In Genesis we see man ruined, in Exodus man redeemed, in Leviticus man worshiping.

Minimum Daily Requirements/Spiritual Vitamins
Sunday: Burnt offering (Lev. 1)
Monday: The priests (Lev. 8)
Tuesday: Pure food laws (Lev. 11)
Wednesday: The Day of Atonement (Lev. 16)
Thursday: The feasts of Jehovah (Lev. 23)
Friday: God's pledge (Lev. 26)
Saturday: Dedication (Lev. 27)

Numbers and Mumblers

This book might be called the "Wilderness Wandering." Numbers is also called the "Book of the March" and the "Roll Call." It might also be called the "Book of Murmurings" because from beginning to end it is filled with the spirit of rebellion against God. Read what God says about this in Psalm 95:10.

Numbers is indeed the book of the wilderness, recording the pitiable failure of Israel at Kadesh-barnea, and the consequent wanderings and experiences of the people in the wilderness. It records the pilgrimage, warfare, service and failure of the nation after the Exodus from Egypt. This, however, is not all the message of Numbers. The first 10 chapters give us the divine legislation; chapters 11—20 tell the story of the nation's failure; but the closing chapters of the book records Israel's return to Jehovah's favor and final victory, even in the wilderness.

In 1 Corinthians 10, we learn that the things which happened to them were "examples" for us. In other

40

words their whole history was an "object lesson" to us, illustrating God's dealing with us today.

We are not saved by good works but we are saved for good works (Eph. 2:10). The law can bring us to the land of promise but only our divine Joshua (Christ) can bring us in. Paul says that the law is the schoolmaster to bring us to Christ (Gal. 3:24).

Leviticus deals with the believer's worship; Numbers deals with the believer's walk. In Leviticus we see the believer's privileges; in Numbers the wilderness is the drill field.

If you know five names, you will master the story of the Book of Numbers:

Moses, the great leader.

Aaron, the high priest, Moses' brother.

Miriam, who was Moses' and Aaron's sister.

Joshua and Caleb, the two spies who dared to believe God, the only men of their generation who lived to enter Canaan.

GOD'S SCHOOL

The children of Israel learned:

1. That they must trust God and not man in the day of crisis (Ps. 37:5). Read Numbers 13:26—14:24.
2. That God would supply all their need according to His riches (Phil. 4:19). He gave them food (Num. 11:7-9), meat (11:31-33), water (20:8), leaders and a Promised Land.
3. That they must worship God according to His instructions.

PREPARATION FOR THE JOURNEY Numbers 1–12

Numbers opens with the children of Israel in the

41

wilderness of Sinai. The Law had been given, the Tabernacle had been built, and the priests had been assigned to their service. Now God was going to prepare the nation for its work.

Order is heaven's first law. We see God numbering and arranging the tribes (chaps. 1 and 2), choosing and assigning duties to the priests and Levites (chaps. 3 and 4). God is the author of order.

In the first chapter, Moses is commanded to take a census. The Lord knows by name those who are His (2 Tim. 2:19; Phil. 4:3). The thought of God numbering His people and gathering them about Himself is most precious to our hearts. He dwelt in the camp. The 12 tribes surrounded the Tabernacle of the Lord. The Levites encamped directly around the court, and Moses, Aaron and the priests guarded the entrance whereby God was approached.

The circumference of the camp is supposed to have been 12 miles. What an imposing sight the camp must have been. Think of 600,000 men, 20 years old and upward, and about 3 million women and children in this great camp! But the most glorious thing was that God was in their midst.

GOD WAS THERE

Here were about three million people on a sterile desert, not a blade of grass, not a drop of water. How were they to be fed? God was there! How were they to trace their way through a howling wilderness where there was no path? God was there! God was their night lamp and their day shade.

No one had gone before to blaze a trail for the children of Israel. There was not a footprint, not a landmark. It is much like our life as a Christian today. We would not know where to walk except for one little sentence from the lips of the Lord, *I am the way* (John 14:6). He will guide us step by step. There is no uncertainty, for He said, *He who follows Me shall not walk in the darkness* (John 8:12).

God gave His children a cloud to guide them by day and a pillar of fire by night. It is interesting to see how they were guided a step at a time. They did not know when they were to go and when to stop, but the pillar of cloud was always leading (Num. 9:17).

Sin crept into this well-ordered camp life. The people began to murmur against God. God sent judgment of fire (11:1-3). Then they complained about their food (11:4). It seemed monotonous. They longed for the garlic and onions of Egypt. As a result of their complaining, God sent them quails for 30 days. They made gluttons of themselves and many became ill and died (11:32-34).

Then we read of the sin of Aaron, the high priest, and Miriam, the sister of Moses. God had chosen Moses to be the leader of this great people and Aaron and Miriam were only his assistants. Jealousy crept into their hearts. They wanted more honor. Read of Miriam's terrible punishment. She was smitten with leprosy for seven days (12:1-16).

WILDERNESS WANDERINGS Numbers 13—20

After one year at Mount Sinai the Israelites journeyed to Kadesh. This is at the southern border of the Promised Land. The children of Israel could have gone into the land of promise immediately had it not been for the sin of unbelief.

43

When the spies came back and told them about the giants in the land and the high-walled cities, their hearts failed them. They would not listen to Joshua and Caleb who agreed with all that was told, but added, *We should by all means go up and take possession of it, for we shall surely overcome it* (13:30). But the people would not trust God. They said, *Let us . . . return to Egypt* (14:4).

When they refused to enter Canaan, the door was closed to them. It meant wandering in the wilderness for 40 years. God said that He would not allow any of those who were over 20 years old to enter Canaan, except Joshua and Caleb.

God opens doors and no man closes, and He closes doors and no man opens (Isa. 22:22; Rev. 3:8). God opened the door and about three million souls walked out of Egypt; He closed the door when the Egyptians tried to follow.

God took the children of Israel out of Egypt so that He could take them into Canaan, the land of promise. God did not want the children of Israel just to come out of Egypt. He wanted to have them come into the Promised Land. But as we have already seen, their fear disqualified them to take over the land of promise.

Often it is our fear that keeps us from enjoying all that God wants to give us. We fear what others will say. We fear what might happen if we put our trust completely in Christ. We start out with high hope in the enthusiasm of our first love. Yonder lies the land of possibilities and achievement. Then the giants appear—giants of opposition from without; giants of fear from within. Our faith fails. We forget God. We compare our difficulties with our own strength rather than committing them to God. Then we turn back into the wilderness of half trust, half victory and whole despair.

Numbers 33 is the pitiful log book of this journey. Going, going, pitching, and departing but never arriving anywhere. An endless circle of aimless wandering with no success. They did not travel all the time but remained in some places with their flocks and herds grazing on the surrounding hills. When the cloud lifted, they marched. They finally approached Canaan from the east of the Dead Sea.

Think of the lost years from Kadesh back to Kadesh because men would not believe God. When we doubt God we find this to be our experience, too. We feel defeated and discouraged. We wander around but never accomplish anything. It is like a revolving door—lots of motion but getting no place.

Before this scene ends we find Israel murmuring again, this time because of the shortage of water. They complained bitterly to Moses and Aaron and said they wished they had never left Egypt. The land was dry and parched and there was no water to drink. Moses and Aaron again went to God. He told Moses to take his rod and speak to the rock before the people, and the rock would give forth water.

Moses' patience was at an end. The people had complained about everything. In anger he called the people rebels and instead of speaking to the rock he struck it. The water gushed out. Even though Moses disobeyed, God kept His promise and provided water.

Is it not sad that even children of God fail under

45

testing? Moses' error was great, yet it showed him to be just like us. Moses put himself up as God (20:10). This dishonored Jehovah God. Because Moses smote the rock a second time (see first time, Exod. 17:5,6) instead of speaking to it, he was not permitted to enter the Promised Land. Christ, like the rock, was to be smitten once for our sins (1 Cor. 10:4). He need not be smitten again.

ON TO CANAAN Numbers 21—36

By Numbers 21 all the Israelites who had left Egypt had died except Moses, Aaron, Joshua, Caleb, Miriam and those who were under 20 years of age when the spies entered the land. Finally, while they were in Kadesh, Miriam, Moses' sister, and Aaron, his brother, now over 100 years old, died.

Israel was to move on again. They started from Kadesh-barnea, this time with faces set resolutely toward the land of promise. The way was difficult, much harder than before, but faith had been renewed, discipline had done its work, and the arm of God went forth conquering.

Israel was soon complaining again, although over and over again God had proven to them that His way is best. Discontent and murmuring seem to have been ingrained habits of the children of Israel. Grumbling is the easiest thing in the world to learn.

The Israelites battled with the Canaanites and became discouraged. Then they grumbled because they had to march around the land of Edom instead of through it. They growled again against God and against Moses because they disliked the manna (Num. 21:5).

This time God sent fiery serpents among the people, which caused suffering and death. After they confessed their sin, Moses prayed for the deliverance of his people. God did not take away the serpents but told Moses to make a brass serpent and fasten it to a pole so that all could see it. As soon as they looked, they would live (21:6-9).

The Bible reveals that the whole human family has felt the serpent's sting of sin which means death. The only way man can live is by looking to the One who took upon Himself the likeness of men and was lifted up on the cross to take the sting of death upon Himself. If we look on Him, our Saviour, we shall live (John 3:14-15).

Minimum Daily Requirements/Spiritual Vitamins
Sunday: The guiding cloud (Num. 9:15-23)
Monday: The report of the spies (Num. 13:16-33)
Tuesday: Israel's unbelief (Num. 14:1-45)
Wednesday: Water from the rock (Num. 20:1-13)
Thursday: The brazen serpent (Num. 21:1-9)
Friday: Balaam's beast (Num. 22:1-41)
Saturday: The cities of refuge (Num. 35:6-34)

Deuteronomy, Moses' Last Speech

Deuteronomy shows the blessings of obedience and the curse of disobedience. Everything depends on obedience—life itself, possession of the Promised Land, victory over foes, prosperity and happiness. This book also teaches the inflexibility of the law.

Deuteronomy is a collection of orations Moses gave as his farewell to the children of Israel. It is a Book of Remembrance. The name Deuteronomy means "second law" which indicates that the law is repeated. Moses reminded the people what God had done for them and what they were to do to serve Him when they reached the Promised Land. It omits the things that relate to the priests and Levites and includes the things that the people should know.

You will come to appreciate the full force and magnetic beauty of Deuteronomy only as you read its pages. Read it through in a single sitting.

Nothing in literature matches its eloquence; nothing in the Old Testament has more powerful appeal for the spiritual life. No book in the Word of God

pictures better the life which is lived according to
God's will and the blessings showered upon the soul
who comes into the richness and fullness of spiritual
living along the rugged pathway of simple obedience.

Jesus often quoted from Deuteronomy. He answered the devil in the hour of temptation from its
writings (Matt. 4:4,7,10; also Deut. 8:3; 6:13,16).

LOOKING BACK Deuteronomy 1—4

How deplorable is unbelief! God never fails us
when we trust in Him, but He cannot do many
mighty works because of our unbelief (Matt. 13:58).

Several hundred years before, God had promised
to Abraham and his seed a rich and wondrous land
(Gen. 17:8). Now they were ready to enter in after all
the years of anticipation and hope. As we shall see,
God is putting the conditions of their entering and
holding the land before the children of Israel in
Deuteronomy. We see all these conditions summed
up in one great word: obedience.

The Book of Deuteronomy is one long plea for
obedience to God based on two grand motives of love
and fear (Deut. 10:12). In the first four books of the
Pentateuch God chose Israel. Now He is letting Israel choose Him.

Only Caleb and Joshua were left from that generation that had come out of Egypt. All the others had
died. The younger men who now lived had suffered
hardships in the wilderness wanderings and were
ready and anxious for conquest! But Moses' work is
finished, for God has told him another will lead them
into Canaan (Num. 20:12).

Moses gave the children of Israel a look back. He

recalled their history and reviewed their wanderings. He reminded them of God's faithfulness and urged them to be grateful and obedient. He likened God's care of them to a loving father who cherishes his little ones. He supplied all their needs; they lacked nothing (Deut. 2:7). Moses spoke to his beloved people in the most earnest and eloquent way and appealed to them to serve and obey God.

Moses' work was done. He had spent the last 40 years delivering his people from the bondage of Egypt and guiding them through the dangers that confronted them. He trained them, gave them forms of government, laws, religious institutions and molded them into a nation. The children of Israel were now at the end of their journey, in the plain east of the Jordan overlooking the land they had come so far to possess. The Israelites were like young men leaving school or college, and about to enter upon their life's work.

LOOKING UP Deuteronomy 5—26

In Deuteronomy 12:1 we see the key to this section. God wanted to teach Israel the love which is the real fulfilling of the law (Rom. 13:8-10; Matt. 22:37-40).

Moses set forth the law simply and clearly so that it would take a living hold of the people. God says, "You are my people; I love you. I have chosen you; I am in the midst of you. I will protect you. I am only asking you to obey me for your good." He says *Be holy; for I am holy.* Since God's people are His, He wants them to walk in the world in the way that befits them, separating themselves from evil (Deut. 14).

They should show charity toward each other (chap. 15). They must gather together to worship (chap. 16).

God showed the Israelites that they were to be thankful, yes, really thankful. They were to be full of joy and gladness. Why shouldn't they be joyful in the best land on earth, and with such a God as Jehovah? Surely they ought to be glad and love their God with all their heart.

LOOKING OUT Deuteronomy 27—33

Moses gave the people some solemn warnings. He first spoke of the blessings that the children of Israel could enjoy if they would be obedient. Deuteronomy 28 is a most remarkable chapter. It traces what Israel might have been through obedience (vv. 1-14) and is yet to be in the millennial age to come (Isa. 60—62; Zech. 14:8-21; Jer. 31:1-9; Deut. 30:1-10; Rom.11: 25-31). He then told them the results of disobedience. Misfortune would follow them in everything they would undertake—in business, in farming, and in health. They would suffer for their disobedience to God.

Moses spoke to Joshua, his personal attendant through the wilderness. He was one of the spies who dared to believe God. He was now 80 years old and Moses committed to him the leadership of this great people! Read his words in Deuteronomy 31:7,8.

This grand old man, 120 years of age, stood as a witness to the grace of God. Moses had celebrated the deliverance of Israel from Egypt with a song (Exod. 15), and now he closed his life's work with another (Deut. 32). He wrote a third which we know as Psalm 90.

After the song and final words of blessing, Moses went up to Nebo's heights and there God showed him the Promised Land toward which his face had so long been set. Moses died there and God buried His servant in the valley. God buries the workman but carries on the work.

Minimum Daily Requirements/Spiritual Vitamins
Sunday: Forward march (Deut. 1:6-46)
Monday: Instructions (Deut. 5:1-33; 6:4-18)
Tuesday: The Messiah, Prophet (Deut. 18:15-22)
Wednesday: God's covenant (Deut. 30:1-20)
Thursday: The song of Moses (Deut. 32:1-44)
Friday: God's blessings (Deut. 33:1-29)
Saturday: The death of Moses (Deut. 34:1-12)

Joshua and the Conquest

2

The Book of Joshua begins the second division of the Old Testament, the books of History. No book has more encouragement and wisdom for the soldier of the cross than Joshua. It is full of spiritual truth.

Joshua is the "Book of Conquest" or the "Battlefield of the Canaan Heritage." It goes on where Deuteronomy leaves off. The chosen people were led out of bondage by Moses and into the Promised Land by Joshua.

This book bears the name of Joshua, the hero of this great conquest. The name Joshua was originally Hoshea which means salvation, or Jehoshua, God's salvation. Joshua was the servant of Jehovah, one by whom God issued His orders and by whom He accomplished His purposes—God's prime minister.

This book seems to fall into two great parts. If you can only remember this much of an outline, you will remember the most important things:

A. Conquest of the Promised Land (chaps. 1—12)

B. Occupation of the Promised Land (chaps. 13—24)

MOBILIZATION OF THE ARMY Joshua 1, 2

Open your Bible to Joshua 1. The children of Israel were on the border of the land of promise, near the banks of the Jordan. (Boundaries of the Promised Land as given in Joshua 1:4 were: the Wilderness on the south, Lebanon mountains on the north, Euphrates River on the east, Mediterranean on the west.) We see an anxious crowd of people waiting to enter the land they had been promised. Picture the row on row of tents and all the people wondering when Joshua would say, "Go."

God called Joshua to lead the Israelites into the Promised Land. We have the words which must have come to him in answer to a prayer for help in his great undertaking. *I will be with you; I will not fail you or forsake you* (Josh. 1:5). These words are just as true for us.

God Says Some Very Important Things

1. Be on the move (1:2).
2. Set your foot down (1:3).
3. Take it all (1:4). Not until Solomon's day, some 500 years later, was this fully realized (2 Chron. 9:26), but it was coming all the time.
4. Take the sword, God's Word (Josh. 1:8). The Book of Law was Joshua's Bible. Our Bible is far more complete and we know more about God's will because Christ has interpreted it for us. Do we meditate upon the Word? Do we follow it? Read Joshua 1:7.

5. Go in for a full life (1:11).

We see both Joshua and the people prepared for the journey. Read Joshua 1:16. Remember, Joshua had been one of the 12 spies who had been sent into Canaan 40 years before. This time he sent two scouts to bring a report of the land. Joshua asked them especially to find out the strength of Jericho. This was the first stronghold they would have to attack after crossing the river. It lay on the best route into the central part of the country. In Jericho the spies aroused suspicion but were saved from death by Rahab. Read the story in Joshua 2.

The Canaanites, the people of the land, were the descendants of Canaan, the son of Ham. They were a wicked and idolatrous people. God had warned them in the destruction of Sodom and Gomorrah, but they had not changed a bit. Now God was going to destroy their power and give their land to the Israelites. But Rahab hung a scarlet cord out of her window that her house might be marked and spared when the city was destroyed (Josh. 2:21). We find this woman's name again in the genealogy of Jesus (Matt. 1:5).

FORWARD MARCH Joshua 3—5

Encouraged by the report the spies had brought, the Israelites moved from their camp at Shittim, six miles from the Jordan, to a spot within a mile of the swollen stream. The officers passed through the camp and ordered all to watch the Ark and follow it at a distance of about one-half mile (Josh. 3:4). The children of Israel had followed the cloud in the wilderness. Now they would follow the Ark of the Covenant which represented the presence of God.

The long journey in the desert was over and the mystery of an unknown country and an unknown life lay before them. The great leader, Joshua, instructed the people to sanctify themselves because the next day the Lord would do wonders among them (3:5).

At the beginning of the Exodus from Egypt they crossed the Red Sea. At the close of the Exodus they crossed the Jordan River. Both were memorable events in the history of the children of Israel.

It was the time of the overflow of the Jordan. There were no bridges and only a few fords, and these were not passable. The spies had crossed by swimming, no doubt. But how could a great host with women, children and baggage cross? God had a way. He gave the directions for the people to follow. Martin Luther said, "I know not the way He (Christ) leads me, but well do I know my Guide."

Remember how Christ told the man with the withered arm to do what he could not do—to stretch it forth. The man made the attempt to do the impossible and Christ made it possible. The way to stretch forth the palsied arm was to stretch it forth. The way to cross the Jordan was to cross it. Joshua told the priests to take up the Ark and step into the Jordan, when the river was overflowing all its banks. When the soles of their feet touched the waters of the Jordan, they stood on dry ground. And all Israel passed over on dry ground (3:9-17). With men this is impossible, but with God all things are possible.

God is always doing the impossible. God's biddings are His enablings. A man once said, "If God tells me to jump through a stone wall, it would be my duty to jump; it would be God's duty to remove the wall!" The Israelites followed the Ark, the symbol of the divine Presence. And Christ is the reality of the divine Presence for us (Matt. 28:20). He goes before us and says, "Follow me," and He sends His Holy Spirit to whisper in our ear and say, *This is the way, walk in it* (Isa. 30:21).

The Bible tells us of the crossing of the river. From the river bed, the place where the priests' feet stood firm, the stones were taken and piled up on the other shore as a lasting memorial of the wonders God did for them (Josh. 4:3). No formal prayer is recorded, but memorial stones are set up. The people wanted to perpetuate the memory of their great Deliverer.

THE FALL OF JERICHO Joshua 6

Jericho was not far from the Jordan and about a short 20-minute walk from the encampment at Gilgal.

It was the key to southern Canaan. The walls of Jericho had to come down so the Israelites might proceed to conquer the Promised Land. But how could this be brought about? To the Israelites God's directions seemed strange, but they kept steadily at the part assigned them. What was their task? Read Joshua 6.

The procession of priests, Ark, men and trumpets that marched around the city daily were the only visible means for its capture. But when the people obeyed the command of the Lord given by Joshua, they saw God's power.

The Israelites believed that they were following God's plan. The seven trumpets, leading a procession seven days, and seven times on the seventh day, showed the Israelites that this was Jehovah's plan of conquest as directly as an American flag would inform people today that the property over which it waved was under the protection of the United States. God put an invisible band around the foundation of that city wall and tightened it, and when God does that to the foundation of any structure, national or personal—beware!

It is not hard work that is needed; it is vision. It is easy to blow a trumpet, a little thing to walk around a wall. The hard thing is to see the good in it. Say, "Lord, one step is enough for me."

No one wants long delays. We love to see things, happen. If there must be six days of weary traveling around the walls, the seventh day will come when the walls will fall. God gives victories through ways that seem foolish to us (1 Cor. 1:17-29).

CAMPAIGN AT AI Joshua 7,8

The capture of Jericho gave the Israelites a chance to enter central Canaan. The next strategically important place was Ai, which commanded the entrance into the valley leading into northern Canaan.

As in the case of Jericho, Joshua sent spies to Ai to learn the situation (Josh. 7:3). Then a small force was sent up the steep ascent, but when the garrison at Ai came out and attacked them, the Israelites were defeated. In the disaster all saw the withdrawal of God's guiding hand. They soon learned that they could not trust in their own strength alone. Furthermore, one man's sin caused Israel's defeat. Israel had become a nation and no one could act alone. Achan had hidden a wedge of gold. Read the story in Joshua

7. Achan alone was guilty, yet the nation suffered (Josh. 7:11).

SOUTHERN CAMPAIGN Joshua 9,10

The Israelites went a second time to Ai. This time they were victors. The taking of Ai shows good military strategy. In working for the Lord we must recognize the value of the best in human reason, but strategy without obedience is worth nothing. Moody said, "Work as if everything depended upon you, and pray as if everything depended upon God."

The fame of Israel began to spread far and wide. The kings of Canaan formed a league against the oncoming hosts. But Joshua routed the allied army. Read about the hail storm and the prolonged daylight which God sent to help His warriors (Josh. 10:10,11, 13).

NORTHERN CAMPAIGN Joshua 11

After southern Canaan was in Israel's possession, a new confederacy had to be faced and conquered. The northern kings had joined together to break the power of the conquering Israelites. But in divine strength Joshua routed them all. This did not all happen at once. Scripture says that it took *a long time*. At last the land rested from war (11:23).

Until recently it was supposed that Canaan was at this time a country of semi-barbarians. Now we know that as early as 3500 B.C. Canaan was subject to Babylonian rulers, and the Babylonian language and civilization had been adopted. Next came Egyptian domination, and we know the high culture of Egypt. Many of the Tell-el-Amarna tablets, dating 1400 B.C., before the conquest of Canaan by the Israelites, are letters to the Pharaoh of Egypt written in the Babylonian language by tributary princes in Canaan. At that period Canaan already had a long civilized past.

DIVISION OF THE LAND Joshua 13—24

Joshua was an old man now, about 90 years old, and he realized that the conquest of the land was by no means complete. There yet remained *much ... land to be possessed.* In order that the children of Israel might do this, he divided it among them.

"This is Judah's; this is Asher's; and this is Simeon's ...." They said this even while the Amorites, the Jebusites, and the Hittites possessed the Promised Land (Josh. 13). The division of the land was made by faith in certain things which under God's guidance they proposed to do in the long struggle that followed.

Unless we keep a vision before us and dream dreams, we will never win either materially or spiritually. This is just what the Israelites did. They reached out into a hoped-for but unknown future when they divided up territory which was still in the hands of their foes! It was not all conquered until the time of David. All that was subdued at this time was the mountains; the cities and plains were hardly touched.

CALEB'S POSSESSION Joshua 14

Caleb now was 85 years old! Joshua and he had been alone among the spies because they had dared to trust God! How many spies did Moses send into Canaan? How many of their names do you remember? No doubt these two are the only ones. Two trusted God and these are the only names we know. As a reward for obedience, these were the only ones in their generation who were permitted to enter Canaan, the Promised Land.

Caleb asked his friend Joshua for the high and walled cities! (Josh. 14:12.) Caleb was old but he gloried in the hardness of the task. One of Helen Keller's teachers said she was the happiest person she had ever met even though she was deaf, dumb and blind. Her teacher attributed it to her having overcome so much. Caleb was the happiest man in the camp because he had overcome so much and yet had fields to conquer!

The Lord has never promised His children they will have an easy time serving Him. In fact, Christ said, *In the world you have tribulation* (John 16:33). The promise is not for ease; it is for victory. Christ says, *I have overcome the world.* We grow in adversity, for we learn to trust the Lord more. Paul said to Timothy, *Suffer hardship ... as a good soldier of Christ Jesus* (2 Tim. 2:3).

"General Booth, tell me what has been the secret of your success all the way through," begged Dr. J. Wilbur Chapman of the head of the Salvation Army.

Slowly General Booth replied, "I will tell you the secret. God has had all there was of me."

JOSHUA'S FAREWELL Joshua 24

Joshua was an old man. He knew that he could not live much longer. He wanted to give the people some last words of admonition. He called the leaders and all the people together and urged them to remember the power and faithfulness of God and admonished them to be faithful to Him (24:14,15).

It is a good thing to have people make an open confession and commit themselves to a solemn promise. These older men who had made an open confession were true to their promises. It is a great help for young people to stand and make a public confession of Christ and unite with the church. You have made a definite commitment which gives you something to live up to.

At 110 years of age the grand old man, Joshua, died. We see three graves. Joshua's, the great leader of Israel; Eleazer's, the priest; and Joseph's, whose bones the children of Israel had carried with them from Egypt and which were now buried in the land of promise. Here is a great tribute to a great leader, *And Israel served the Lord all the days of Joshua* (Josh. 24:31).

Minimum Daily Requirements/Spiritual Vitamins
Sunday: Joshua's commission (Josh. 1,2)
Monday: Crossing the Jordan (Josh. 3)
Tuesday: The fall of Jericho (Josh. 6)
Wednesday: The sin of Achan (Josh. 7)
Thursday: Occupation of the land (Josh. 11)
Friday: Caleb's possession (Josh. 14)
Saturday: Joshua's farewell (Josh. 24)

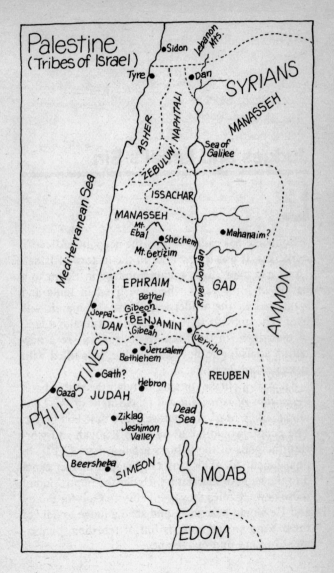

Palestine
(Tribes of Israel)

SYRIANS

Sidon

Lebanon Mts.

Tyre

Dan

ASHER

MANASSEH

NAPHTALI

ZEBULUN

Sea of
Galilee

Mediterranean Sea

ISSACHAR

MANASSEH

Mt.
Ebal

Shechem

Mahanaim?

Mt. Gerizim

EPHRAIM

GAD

River Jordan

AMMON

Bethel

Gibeon

Joppa

BENJAMIN

DAN

Gibeah

Jericho

Jerusalem

Bethlehem

PHILISTINES

Gath?

Hebron

REUBEN

Gaza

JUDAH

Ziklag

Dead
Sea

Jeshimon
Valley

Beersheba

SIMEON

MOAB

EDOM

63

Judges and Israel's Sin

Someone has called Judges the account of Israel's dark ages. It was a new hour in the history of Israel. Israel had come from a long bondage in Egypt to a period of forty years when she lived in tents and wandered in the wilderness. Now the march was over. The nomads were to become settlers in a land of their own. In the Book of Judges we see a new nation adjusting to her national life. It is filled with struggle and disasters.

There is a phrase running through the whole book —*the sons of Israel did evil in the sight of the Lord* (Judg. 2:11). Mark this phrase every time you find it. The people would fall away from Jehovah and worship the gods of the nations around them (2:13). In punishment for their sins God would deliver them into the hand of that nation. Under the oppression of these new enemies they would cry to God for mercy and He would hear them and send a judge to deliver them. And so the book is full of rebellion, punishment, misery and deliverance.

The book begins with compromise and ends with confusion. This is what happens in every unsurrendered life! After one has read Judges, he may think that all of these years were spent in rebellion and sin. But if you read it carefully, you will see that only about 100 of these years were spent in disloyalty to God. One thing we learn in the Book of Judges is that a people who spend much of their time in disobedience to God make little progress during their lifetime.

There are 15 judges. The chief ones were Deborah, Gideon, Samson and Samuel. There were three types of judges: the warrior judge (Gideon and Samson); priest-judge (Eli); prophet-judge (Samuel). Just how long these judges ruled we do not know. It was probably several hundred years. They were probably raised up as deliverers on different occasions, in different parts of the land and there could have been overlapping of the times of their rules.

Study carefully the following:

1. The wickedness of the human heart (Judg. 2:11-13,17,19; 8:33-35; 10:6; 13:1).

2. God's use of weak people (1 Cor. 1:26-29).
   Notice left-handed assassin Ehud (Judg. 3);
   Shamgar, a rustic with an oxgoad (Judg. 3:31);
   Gideon, from an obscure family (Judg. 6);
   Gideon's little pitcher-armed band (Judg. 7);
   Deborah, a woman (Judg. 4).

3. The Holy Spirit in Judges. Read about
   Othniel—(see Judg. 3:10).
   Gideon—(see Judg. 6:34).
   Jephthah—(see Judg. 11:29).
   Samson—(see Judg. 13:25; 14:6; 15:14).

The critics of the Bible would have the history of God's chosen people start in these dark days of the judges as a wild, lawless, nomadic people who developed finally into a higher civilization. Just because Israel failed to keep God's law does not mean there was no law. Because the people of today's world disregard God's laws and put aside the teachings of Christ, it does not prove that these words were never spoken. Men would love to believe that man's trend is upward. But God's Word shows us plainly that the natural course is downward.

ISRAEL'S FAILURE Judges 1—3:4

Joshua had died (1:1). Much of the Promised Land waited to be conquered. The first act of Israel was to seek God's will as to how they should commence the final conquest. God appointed Judah, the kingly tribe (1:2). The work began in earnest but it ended in weakness.

The people did not obey God and drive out the enemy as God had commanded. Chapter 1 records a series of disobediences. So, of course, chapter 2 is a chapter of defeat and failure. God gave them up to their own will (2:2,3). The children of Israel brought on their own judgment and became their own executioners.

Sometimes we wonder why God didn't remove all the enemies from the Promised Land before He let the children of Israel go in. But God had a reason (Judg. 3:1-4). God uses the results of our lack of faith in Him to prove to us our sin and weakness, and He allows our weakness to drive us back to Him.

God wanted the chosen people to realize that they

were a holy people. They must not mix with the wicked nations about them. Christians today must remember that they cannot mix with the world. They must keep close to God and war against sin and unrighteousness. God wants us to be good warriors. Read Ephesians 6:10-18 and see the armor He provides.

And so toleration toward a people that were utterly corrupt resulted in the undoing of God's people. See the result, Judges 2:20-22.

THE JUDGES Judges 3:5—16:31

Joshua had no successor. After his death, each tribe acted independently. There was no capital and no fixed government. There was no unity of action except in the time of danger, when the tribes combined for their own good. When the people sinned against God, their enemies defeated them and ruled them. When in their distress they sought the Lord, He sent great leaders called judges, who delivered them. God was always near His people, and when they cried, He answered. He promises us that He will never leave us nor forsake us.

In Judges we see the patience of God and His constant readiness to respond to the least sign of penitence in His people (Judg. 3:9,15; 4:3-7; 6:6-12; 10:15,16). He repeated His mercy again and again although it was never appreciated.

First Apostasy Judges 3:7-11

The Israelites settled among the Syrian nations. But they were too ready to live at peace with these other nations and yielded too much for the sake of peace. Read Judges 3:5-8 to see what they did. They intermarried to make their position safer. They traded with the Amorites, Hivites, Perizzites. They set boundary lines to make things run smoothly. Next they accepted their neighbor's religion (3:7) and then his bad customs. But soon the Mesopotamians oppressed them (3:8). The Israelites then realized that they had left the God whose presence had assured them victory. For eight years they were under the oppression and year by year conditions grew worse.

God sent help from the south in answer to their cry (3:9). The deliverer was Othniel, Caleb's nephew. No doubt he had frequent skirmishes with the Arab marauders from the wilderness (3:10). First he prayed, then went out to battle. When we see an army bow in prayer as the Swiss did at Morat, the Scots at Bannockburn and General MacArthur's troops in the Philippines, we have faith in their spirit and courage for they are feeling their dependence on God!

Othniel, the first of the judges, was one of the best. Othniel's first concern was to put away the idolatry of Israel and teach them the law of the Lord and remind them of their calling as a nation. Soon success and victory was theirs (3:10,11). He pointed Israel to a higher reverence for God and His plans. Forty years of rest followed.

Second Apostasy Judges 3:12-31

God used different kinds of men to deliver His people. Israel's second judge, Ehud, is in marked contrast to Othniel. The long peace which the country enjoyed after the Mesopotamian army had been driven out let the people lapse again into spiritual weakness (3:12). This time the Moabites led the attack. The punishment lasted for 18 years. Again the people cried to God, and Ehud, with whom Shamgar's name is associated, was the deliverer judge (3:15). This left-handed Benjamite chose his own method of action and assassinated the Moabite king. But 80 years of rest for Israel followed (3:30). Shamgar, the man of the oxgoad, followed next in line (3:31).

Third Apostasy Judges 4,5

Next a prophetess arose in Israel (Judg. 4:4). She was one of those rare women whose heart burns with enthusiasm when men's hearts are despondent. Many a queen has reigned with honor and wisdom, and often a woman's voice has struck a deep note which has roused nations.

Israel had been oppressed for 20 years (Judg. 4:3). The oppression was terrible under Sisera. Again they cried and God heard. This time the story of deliverance was filled with romance and song. Together Deborah and Barak delivered Israel from their oppression. The land was so filled with Canaanite spoilers that the highways could not be used. War was everywhere, and the Israelites were defenseless and crushed; but God delivered them.

After Jabin, king of Canaan, was defeated and his 900 chariots turned into ploughshares, we might expect that Israel would at last know the danger of leaving God. Without God they were as weak as babes. Will they not now bend themselves to Him? Not yet. But Deborah's work was not in vain. She destroyed the heathen altars and improved the land.

Everywhere they ploughed new ground, built houses, repaired roads, and they had 40 years of rest. But . . . .

Fourth Apostasy Judges 6—8:32

Then a fourth apostasy came (6:1). For seven years the Midianites held the Israelites under bondage so terrible that the people hid themselves in caves in the mountains (6:2). Again they cried unto the Lord. Gideon, a humble farmer, was called to act as deliverer. He broke down the altar of Baal and restored the worship of God. The story of Gideon and his band of 300 men with their pitchers and horns is one of the most fascinating in history. Refresh yourself with this story (7:7-24).

After the great victory over the Midianites, Israel sought to make Gideon king but he refused. Gideon was not perfect. We find in the record some things that he should not have done. But he did have faith that God could honor, and God gave his name a place in the Hall of Faith in Hebrews 11.

Fifth Apostasy Judges 8:33—10:5

Gideon was one of the most successful judges to maintain order. But no sooner was Gideon's funeral over than discord began. A fifth time we see the people falling into the sin of idolatry by worshiping the Baals (8:33). There was no good ruler to follow Gideon. He left many sons but not one of them could take his place. Abimelech, a son of Gideon, unprincipled and brutal, secured the allegiance of the men at Shechem and ruled three years in tyranny. He was slain by a woman and a period of 45 years of quietness followed under the dictatorship of Tola and Jair.

Sixth Apostasy Judges 10:6—12:15

In the sixth apostasy we find the people almost entirely given over to idolatry. Their condition was appalling. God sent judgment this time from the Philistines for 18 years. At last they cried to God. For the first time it is recorded that He refused to hear them and reminded them of how repeatedly He had delivered them (10:13). The true attitude of Jehovah toward them is found in Judges 10:16.

Deliverance came through Jephthah. Jephthah was a man of heroic daring. Read the story of his vows and victories, especially the vow that he made concerning his only child (11:30-40). After his great victory Jephthah judged Israel only six years.

Seventh Apostasy Judges 13—16

The seventh apostasy opens with the words of Judges 13:1. This time they were disciplined by the Philistines under whose awful oppression they lived 40 years. Here we read the story of Samson—a story filled with opportunity and failure.

In those days everything was dependent upon physical strength. That was what made a leader great. Hence, everything should have been in Samson's favor, but he entered into an unholy alliance which meant his downfall. The final fall occurred at Gaza. (Read Judg. 16.) Nothing is more pathetic than Samson, blind and bound, grinding in the house of the Philistines, when he ought to have been delivering his nation from them (16:20,21).

THE APPENDIX Judges 17—21

These last chapters give us a picture of anarchy and

confusion. Israel had forsaken God. We find confusion in the religious (Judg. 17,18), moral (Judg. 19), and political (Judg. 21) life of the nation. These events also give us a picture of the internal condition of the chosen people. The story of the backsliding of individuals is followed by the backsliding of the nation.

The history of the church through the ages has been like this with Luther, Knox, and Wesley as deliverers. The biography of many a common Christian is like this too. God opens doors and gives us grace for great tasks. Then we forget Him and begin to have our interests in the world about us. This brings loss and defeat. But God hears our cry of repentance and restores us to favor again.

Understanding Ruth

This delightful story should be read in connection with the first chapters of Judges as no doubt it gives us an idea of the domestic life of Israel during the rule of Gideon or Jephthah. No one knows where or when it was written. This book, written on a separate scroll, was read at Pentecost, the harvest festival.

Ruth was the great-grandmother of David. This book tells of the beginning of the messianic family within the messianic nation into which over a thousand years later the Messiah was to be born.

There are some interesting things to notice in this book. Ruth was a Moabitess. These people were descendants of Lot and were heathen. God, in establishing the family which was to produce the world's Saviour, chose a beautiful heathen girl, led her to Bethlehem and made her the bride of Boaz. Of course, we know that although Ruth was born a heathen, through her first husband or Naomi she learned of the true God.

Boaz was the son of Rahab, the harlot found in Jericho (see Matt. 1:5). So we see that David's great-grandmother was a Moabitess and his great-grandfather was half Canaanite. This is found in the bloodline of the Messiah. This is God's grace. He adopts the Gentiles into Christ's family.

Minimum Daily Requirements/Spiritual Vitamins
Sunday: Only partial victories (Judg. 1—2:5)
Monday: Times of the judges (Judg. 2:16—3:11)
Tuesday: Deborah and Barak (Judg. 4:4—5:31)
Wednesday: Gideon (Judg. 6:1-16; 7:16-25)
Thursday: Jephthah's vow (Judg. 11:12-40)
Friday: Samson, the strong man (Judg. 15 and 16)
Saturday: The story of Ruth (Book of Ruth)

The Tragedy of Saul
(1 Samuel)

The Book of Samuel begins the five hundred year period of the kings of Israel (approximately 1095-586 B.C.). The long period of the rule of the judges ends with Samuel. When Samuel came into power, the people were in an awful state. They had practically rejected God, and were clamoring for an earthly king (1 Sam. 8:4-7).

The events recorded in 1 Samuel cover a period of about 115 years from the childhood of Samuel through the troublous times of Saul to the beginning of the reign of David, the king whom God chose. In the personal lives of these three men this book gives us an exceedingly graphic picture of these times. The record brings us up to the time when David is ready permanently to establish the monarchy and God is ready permanently to establish David's throne (Ps. 89).

The book may be divided under the names of its chief characters—Samuel (1—7), Saul (8—15), and David (16—31). This book, of course is named for its most prominent figure, Samuel. Probably he wrote the greater part of it through chapter 24. Nathan and Gad finished it (1 Chron. 29:29 and 1 Sam. 10:25).

SAMUEL, THE KING MAKER 1 Samuel 1—7

Samuel—"asked of God!" That is the meaning of his name. This book opens with the record of Hannah, Samuel's mother, praying for a son whom God could use. Samuel, the last of the judges, was God's answer to this prayer.

Throughout Samuel's long and useful life, he was God's man. He was preeminently a man of prayer. This first book which bears his name is a marvelous study in the place and power of prayer. He was a child of prayer (1 Sam. 3:1-19); he brought victory to his people through prayer (7:5-10); when the nation wanted a king, Samuel prayed unto the Lord (8:6); intercessory prayer was the keynote of his life (12:19-23).

When Samuel was born, Hannah brought him to the Tabernacle at Shiloh. Although the corruption of the priesthood was appalling, Samuel was protected and grew in the fear of the Lord (1 Sam. 3:21).

Read 1 Samuel 3:21. God revisited Shiloh! For Shiloh, the place of worship, had been turned into a place of feasting and dancing (Judg. 21:19-21), and God's presence had left. (Shiloh was the location of the house of God from the days of Joshua to Samuel. Later David moved it to Jerusalem.)

Eli was both judge and priest at that time. He had ruled 40 years. Eli was an indulgent father and as a result his two sons, Hophni and Phinehas, also priests, were allowed to act in a most disgraceful manner. As a result there was moral corruption, and God warned Eli of the downfall of his house.

Fungus growth in a tree usually is not detected for a long time. Everything seems right outwardly; but when the crash suddenly comes, the state of the tree is seen. Israel had been sinning for a long time. At length catastrophe came. During the next invasion of the Philistines, Israel was defeated, the Ark was taken and Eli's sons were killed. When the priest Eli heard all this, the old man, now 98 years of age, died of the shock.

Philistine Conquest

Read the history of the Philistines' possession of the Ark (1 Sam. 5,6). The Philistines were Israel's powerful enemies living to the southwest on the coast. Perhaps this renewed action on their part was due to the death of Samson. When the battle was lost, Israel wondered why God had deserted them. But while warring against God, they asked God to war for them.

After Israel's first defeat by the Philistines they looked to the Ark of God for protection (1 Sam. 4:3-7,10). But the Ark of God was a poor substitute for the God of the Ark. Many people think that when they wear religious symbols, or perform religious rituals, or give money to charitable causes that they will be safe. They think that these things are a charm or talisman to bring them victory.

A Timely Revival

We need a praying band of Christians, a people brought to a sense of their need, and a consecrated preacher to bring about revival. Under the Philistine rule Israel had no definite center of worship. Samuel grew into manhood and assumed the leadership for which he had been born. The first hopeful sign after Israel's long rebellion and defeat was that they had a sense of need. They began to want God.

God cannot do much for people who do not feel that they need anything. God pities those who think they are "all right."

"Well," said Samuel, "if you really mean business, you've got to show me. How? Remove your strange gods" (see 7:3). If you mean business, God will mean business. Religion is not just a matter of emotion but also of the will.

It is often easy for us to "talk big," but it is another question to live up to what we say. We often make promises to God that we never keep. How sad that sometimes our lives shout, "Lie! " to what our lips say.

The people began to lament. Samuel took advantage of this and called on them to return to God and put away their idols. Samuel erected an altar and called it Ebenezer (7:12). Ebenezer means "stone of help. " Christ our victory is called "the stone" in both the Old Testament and the New (Dan. 2:35; Matt. 21:42).

Samuel's Judgeship

In just a brief paragraph we find the story of Samuel's judgeship. His home was at Ramah. From here he was a circuit rider going once a year to Bethel, Gilgal and Mizpah, and overseeing and administering the affairs of the people (1 Sam. 7:15-17).

Samuel was the last of the judges, the first of the prophets and the founder of the monarchy. Beside this, he started a school of the prophets, a kind of seminary, at his home in Ramah. This was the beginning of the "order" of the prophets, or seers. When the Ark was taken, the priests were scattered. Through Samuel, God introduced a new way of dealing with Israel. He called prophets through whom He would speak. It was with Samuel that prophecy became a definite part of the life of Israel.

Samuel's greatest ministry was the organization of the kingdom. The tribes were now going to be formed into a nation. In order to survive among other strong nations, Israel must become powerful.

SAUL, THE KING CHOSEN 1 Samuel 8—15

God never intended Israel to have any king but Himself. He would send them leaders who would receive their orders directly from Him. But Israel had become restless. They wanted a king like the other surrounding nations. We find God granting their request. Here is a great lesson. We either can have God's best or His second best, His directive will or His permissive will.

Saul, Israel's first king, was a failure. He was tall and handsome. He started out splendidly. He proved to be an able military leader. He defeated the enemies about him—the Philistines, the Amalekites and the Ammonites. Saul was humble at first, but we find him becoming proud and disobedient to God. No man had a greater opportunity than Saul and no man ever was a greater failure.

Inasmuch as Saul was granted to Israel as king in

response to Israel's sinful demand, contrary to God's will, did Saul ever really have a chance to "make good" in God's sight? Could he possibly have succeeded under such circumstances? Or was he condemned by God to failure even before he started as king?

We find the answer clearly in God's Word. In 1 Samuel 12:12-15 the prophet of God tells Israel that, although they had demanded their king in defiance of God (v. 12), if both they and their king would fear Jehovah and serve Him, all would be well. The only reason why any soul is ever rejected by God is because that soul has first rejected God. God takes the initiative in love. Man takes the initiative in sin.

Notice Saul's:
1. Presumption at God's altar (13:11-13)
2. Cruelty to his son Jonathan (14:44)
3. Disobedience in the matter of Amalek (15:23)
4. Jealousy and hatred of David (18:29)
5. Sinful appeal to the witch of Endor (28:7).

Saul's Campaigns
1. Against the Ammonites
   Beginning of reign ... unsurmountable obstacles ... army mobilized with great haste ... Ammonites ruined ... Saul's prestige as king strengthened.
2. Against the Philistines
   Saul's sin in assuming function of priest ... God rejected Saul ... Jonathan and single companion created panic among Philistines ... enemy routed.
3. Against the Amalekites

Drove enemy into desert ... marred success by
disobedience ... seized valuable property ...
lied to Samuel ... prophet repeated that God
had rejected him.
4. Against the Philistines
Constant warfare with Philistines ... boy David
met Goliath, giant of Philistines ... slew him ...
panic caused ... David won distinction.
5. Against David
Blind jealousy drove Saul to seek David's life ...
David became an outcast ... David repeatedly
delivered ... Saul, David's enemy till his death
... David's friendship with Saul's son, Jonathan.
6. Against the Philistines
Battlefield plains of Esdraelon ... visit to the
witch of Endor ... defeat and death announced
... Israel completely defeated ... Saul and three
of his sons slain.

Give God His Right-of-Way

All through the years Samuel mourned for Saul.
When he failed, Samuel was faithful in warning him.
Then in loneliness he mourned over him (15:35).

In a battle with the Philistines, Saul and his three
sons met death. Here a life so full of promise ended
in defeat and failure. Saul had not obeyed God abso-
lutely. Think of the difference between the end of
Saul of Tarsus (Paul) and Saul the king! One put God
first, the other himself! God is showing in this book
that He must be all in all; that His children have no
blessing apart from Him.

The morning of Saul's life was bright but soon the
sky became overcast. Then his sun set in the blackest

storm clouds. Follow carefully his rise, his reign, and his ruin.

DAVID, THE KING PROVEN 1 Samuel 16—31

Samuel mourned for Saul but God rebuked him and told him to arise and anoint the new king (16:1).

David, "the apple of God's eye," was one of the great men of all times. He made great contributions to the history of Israel both spiritually and nationally. In 1 Samuel, David is presented as a shepherd lad, a minstrel, an armor bearer, a captain, the king's son-in-law, a writer of psalms, and a fugitive. He was anointed three times and was to be the founder of the royal line of which the King of Kings came.

David, Jesse's son and the great-grandson of Ruth and Boaz, was born in Bethlehem. He was the youngest of eight sons. When David was only 18, God told Samuel to anoint him king to succeed Saul. As a boy he tended his father's sheep, and we read of his brave deeds in defending them from wild beasts.

As a harpist, David's fame reached the king. Saul's melancholy caused David to be called into the court to play. One of the most charming stories of real love in friendship is found between David and Jonathan, Saul's son.

When David was promoted to a high command in the army, his great success roused the jealousy of Saul who determined to kill him. He made several attacks on David's life (1 Sam. 19:10,15,20,21,23,24). But God preserved David. David was delivered from all these dangers. Read David's words in Psalms 59 and 37.

These were trying days for the young man David

who had been appointed to the kingly office. But he was independent and courageous. He learned, too, in those trying days, to trust God, not men. He was an outcast for no wrong that he had done but because of the insane jealousy of Saul. David grew under his trials and afflictions. Instead of letting Saul's hatred harden his heart, he returned love for hate.

Finally David took refuge in flight. During this time Samuel died. Twice Saul's life was in David's hand but both times he spared Saul. Feeling that he should perish one day by the hand of Saul, he took refuge among the Philistines. Psalm 56 was written then.

The closing chapter of our book is draped in black. It gives the closing picture of one of the most disastrous failures. Saul died on the field of battle by his own hand. Advantages and opportunities in youth never guarantee success in manhood. One must keep true to God. Saul's undoing was not so much disobedience, as half-hearted obedience (1 Sam. 15). He was a victim of human pride and jealousy.

Minimum Daily Requirements/Spiritual Vitamins
Sunday: Samuel, "Asked of God" (1 Sam. 1—3)
Monday: Samuel, the prophet (1 Sam. 4—7)
Tuesday: Saul, the king (1 Sam. 8—12)
Wednesday: Saul, the self-willed (1 Sam. 13—15)
Thursday: David anointed (1 Sam. 16—18)
Friday: David's adventures (1 Sam. 19; 20; 22; 24)
Saturday: Death of Samuel and Saul (1 Sam. 25; 26; 31)

The Triumph of David
(2 Samuel)

10

The Book of 1 Samuel records the failure of man's king, Saul. Second Samuel describes the enthronement of God's king, David, and the establishment of the "House of David" through which the Messiah, Jesus Christ, should later come. When Christ comes again, He will sit upon the throne of David (see Isa. 9:7; Luke 1:32).

The link between 1 and 2 Samuel ought to be reviewed. After David had spared Saul (1 Sam. 26), he realized that his life was in danger, and associated himself with the Philistines (1 Sam. 27). Meanwhile, the closing scenes and final tragedy of Saul's life took place (1 Sam. 28—31).

DAVID'S RISE 2 Samuel 1—10

Second Samuel opens when David returned to Ziklag after his great victory over the Amalekites. No doubt he was wondering what had been the outcome of that great battle at Mount Gilboa. His dearest friend Jonathan and King Saul were in that battle. David was not kept in suspense long. An Amalekite from the camp of Israel came running to tell David of the disaster.

David was 30 (2 Sam. 5:4), and never did a man at that age, or any age, act more noble. His generous heart not only forgot all that Saul had done to harm him but remembered all that was favorable in Saul's character. How beautiful is this spirit of forgiveness! See that same spirit when men nailed Christ to the cross (Luke 23:34) and when men stoned a martyr to death (Acts 7:60). David wrote a song for this occasion called "The Song of the Bow." It is filled with extreme tenderness when it speaks of his beloved friend (2 Sam. 1:19-27).

Becoming King

David inquired of God where he should set up his kingdom, and God told him in Hebron. No sooner had David gone to the city than the men of Judah came and anointed him king of Judah. Although it was not all that God had promised David, it was a large installment, for Judah was the royal tribe.

David's start was slow and discouraging, but David had faith in God. He was patient and willing to wait for God to lead. He was humble in his success, and when he sinned he repented. David used every talent God gave him for the glory of his Creator and built up the people of God's choice. He brought Israel to the height of her glory, extending her boundaries from the Mediterranean to the Euphrates. He left a rich heritage—a heritage that included power, wealth, honor, and songs and psalms. But above all he left an example of faithfulness and loyalty to God.

Will we not all adopt David's plan of life? He started right! He began with God. He committed every plan into His keeping (Ps. 37:5). David never forgot that God was supreme. When he sinned, he bowed in penitence and sorrow, and God forgave him.

The men of Judah who came to meet David came to elect him as king. Although he had been anointed privately by Samuel to indicate that God had chosen him, it was natural and necessary to repeat the anointing in public as the outward and visible inauguration of his reign.

However, David's kingship was not acknowledged by all of the people. Abner, the captain of Saul's army, at once took steps to appoint Saul's son king. Civil war followed, but finally everything turned to David and he was made king of all Israel. After seven and one-half years of opposition David finally won the heart of all Israel by his justice and great spirit. He was left now without a rival. Representatives of all the tribes came to Hebron to anoint him king of the whole nation (2 Sam. 5).

In the prime of his life David began the task God intended him to do. He reigned 40 years in all, including 7½ years in Hebron over Judah and 33 years in Jerusalem over the whole land.

David's Reign

The first thing that engaged David as king of Israel was the capture of Jerusalem, the stronghold of Zion. It was an impregnable fortress. David thought it was best suited to be his nation's capital. The record of how for the first time it came completely into the possession of God's people is given in 2 Samuel 5:6-9 and 1 Chronicles 11:4-8.

After David established the capital at Jerusalem, he wanted to bring the Ark of God to the new ruling center, but we are not told that he consulted God. A real tragedy followed (2 Sam. 6:1-10). What do you know of God's directions for carrying the Ark? (See Num. 4:5,15,19,20.) It is not what we think but what God says that is important. Uzzah's opinion was that it was all right to take hold of the Ark to keep it from falling. He was sincere, but it was directly contrary to what God said. He died.

David captured Jerusalem, built it bigger and stronger, conquered the Philistines and unified the people. But all this would have been of little use without putting God at the center. This is really what gave the nation unity and power. Neither a nation nor an individual can be great without Christ in his heart. All the events in David's reign that followed the capture of Jerusalem may be summed up in the words of 1 Chronicles 11:9.

David was an active man and fond of work. His wars with outside nations had ceased. Now he sought to improve and beautify his kingdom. He compared the elegance of his own palace with the Tabernacle where Jehovah dwelt. He thought this difference ought not to be. He called Nathan the prophet and consulted him about building a temple for Jehovah. Read what God told Nathan to tell to David (2 Sam. 7:4-17).

David's spirit is again revealed in his submission to God's plan for him. God did allow him to gather materials for his son to use. God's servants do not take it ill that the Lord thwarts their plans and desires. A real servant learns what God's will is and yields his will to his Master's!

David was powerful in every act of war, although his heart was inclined to peace. Chapter 10 recounts some perilous undertakings. This story gives the closing account of David's rise to power and prepares for the terrible story of his fall.

Under David's rule Israel reached its high-water mark. It has been called Israel's golden age. There were no groves, no idol worship, no worldly functions when "the sweet singer of Israel," the "shepherd boy of Bethlehem," commanded the ship of state. His merchant caravans crossed the deserts and his routes went from the Nile to the Tigris and Euphrates, and Israel prospered in those days. When Israel was right with God, she was invincible against all odds.

David trusted God with all his heart and did not lean on his own understanding. He acknowledged God in all his ways and God directed his path (see Prov. 3:5,6). How did David obtain guidance? By asking for it. Just how God gave the answer we are not told. God has assured us that if we ask He will answer (1 John 5:14,15; Jer. 33:3). God never breaks His word. We have to make decisions almost every hour of our life. Shall I continue this course in my life? Shall my vacation be spent at home, traveling, at rest? Would we take false steps if He made the decisions for us? Could we fail?

DAVID'S FALL 2 Samuel 11—20

We wish the life of David could have ended before chapter 11 was written. In all of God's Word there is no chapter more tragic or more full of warning for the child of God. It tells the story of David's fall. It is like an eclipse of the sun. His sins of adultery and virtual murder were a terrible blot on David's life. He became a broken man. God forgave him but the Word says, "The sword never departed from his house." He reaped just what he had sown. We see the harvest in his own house and in the nation.

Look over the steps in David's fall. You will find the steps downward in rapid succession.

First, he was idle (2 Sam. 11:1,2). It was the time to go to war but David remained in Jerusalem in the place of temptation. At evening time he arose from bed and walked on the roof of his house. He was in that idle, listless mood which opens one to temptation. He saw the beautiful Bathsheba and he wanted her. Ask God to keep your eyes. Refuse the admission of sin into your mind. If David had nipped the temptation in the bud, he would have saved himself a world of agony and awful sin. But instead of driving it out of his mind, he cherished it.

Next, David made inquiry about this woman (2 Sam. 11:3) and then brought her to his house (v. 4).

But the next step was far worse—his sin against Uriah, one of the bravest of his soldiers. And David made Joab his confidant in sin, his partner in murder.

Why do you suppose this tragic story is given in the Bible? It is like a beacon, warning the mariner against some of the most perilous rocks that are to be found in all the sea of life. Don't fool with one sin even in thought. The door may be opened to a lot more. It doesn't take a whole box of matches to start a fire. One will do it!

A year later the prophet Nathan visited David and charged him with his sin. We can imagine the anguish of David's heart when we read of his sincere repentance in Psalm 51. God told David that his child would die because of his sin. See how David accepted this punishment (2 Sam. 12:13-32). When the child died, David arose and worshiped God.

"A living sorrow is worse than a dead one," says a proverb. The death of his child was a grievous sorrow to David, but we cannot imagine the living sorrow which he endured through his beloved son, Absalom. Absalom was a handsome young man, but he was treacherous and weaned away his father's subjects. He sat at the city gate and told the farmers what he would do if he were their ruler. When men bowed in honor, he kissed their hand.

When David left Jerusalem, Absalom gathered his army and marched triumphantly into the city. Finally David prepared for battle with Absalom. During the fray Absalom was caught by his long hair in the trees. Read David's lament over Absalom when he heard the news of his death (2 Sam. 18:19—19:4).

DAVID'S LAST DAYS 2 Samuel 20—24

After the rebellion was crushed, King David returned to his kingdom. New officers were installed and reconstruction began on every hand.

David was a mighty king and warrior. He ranked with Abraham, Moses and Paul. His great spirit is revealed to us in the psalms which he wrote. David sinned, but the story does not end there, because he repented.

This is the *man after God's heart.* We need to

understand David's life in order to understand and use the psalms. We must know, too, why Christ was called the *Son of David* (see Acts 13:22,23).

David had his faults. He did much that was wrong, but he kept his nation from going into idolatry. Although his private sins were grievous, he stood like a rock for Jehovah. David took a chaotic nation and established a dynasty that was to last to the time of the captivity, a period of over 450 years. There never was a greater warrior or statesman than David. He made Israel the dominant power of western Asia.

The last verses of 2 Samuel 24:18-25 tell of King David's buying Araunah's threshing floor. He erected an altar there. This has special significance for it is on this site the great Temple of Solomon was later built. On this sacred spot today stands the Dome of the Rock. It is difficult for the Jews to have this sacred ground dominated by an Islamic shrine.

Minimum Daily Requirements/Spiritual Vitamins
Sunday: David mourns for Jonathan and Saul (2 Sam. 1:1-27)
Monday: David, king of Judah (2 Sam. 2:1-32; 3:1)
Tuesday: David, king of Israel (2 Sam. 5:1-25)
Wednesday: God's promise (2 Sam. 7:1-29)
Thursday: David's sin (2 Sam. 11:1-27)
Friday: David's repentance (2 Sam. 12:1-23; Ps. 51)
Saturday: David and the people (2 Sam. 24:1-17)

From Conquerors to Conquered (Kings and Chronicles)

11

First and Second Kings are a continuation of the Books of Samuel. They cover a period of 400 years and tell the story of the growth and then the decay of the kingdom. We see the kingdom divided and we see both Israel and Judah led into captivity. As their name suggests, the books record the events in the reign of Solomon and the succeeding kings of Judah and Israel. The Southern Kingdom (Judah) had 20 kings, and the Northern Kingdom (Israel) had 19.

Kings opens with David's first successor to the throne of his kingdom, Solomon, and ends with David's last successor, Jehoiachin, released from captivity by the king of Babylon. It opens with the building of the Temple and ends with the Babylonian captivity and the destruction of the Temple.

Kings covers practically the whole rule of the kings over God's chosen people. During Solomon's reign the kingdom reached the height of its grandeur. With the death of Solomon, the kingship ceased to be the medium through which God governed His people. The period of the prophets is introduced at that time by the great Elijah.

THE SPLENDID REIGN OF SOLOMON
1 Kings 1—10

When the book of 1 Kings opens, David was 70. His son Solomon was 19. Adonijah, David's oldest surviving son (2 Sam. 3:4), started a rebellion in an attempt to gain the throne. The prophet Nathan took prompt action against the rebels. David saw that Solomon was the most fit to succeed him and Solomon was God's choice (1 Chron. 22:9; 1 Kings 2:15). Solomon was crowned before David's death (1 Kings 1:30,39,53). The choice of Solomon was popular (1 Kings 1:39,40) and Adonijah soon saw that opposition was useless.

God appeared to Solomon in a dream early in his reign and asked him to choose anything he might wish. The king's wise choice revealed his feeling of inadequacy. He had not been swept off his feet when David twice called him a wise man (1 Kings 2:6-9). Solomon asked for a "hearing heart." Have we a heart that listens to the Lord? God gave him the wisdom for which he asked. What is God's promise to us (Jas. 1:5)?

The greatest undertaking of Solomon's reign was the building of the Temple. This was what his father David had longed to do. The huge stones, the fragrant cedar wood and gold covering gave it unusual splendor. One stone alone was 38 ft. 9 in. long.

There are three earthly temples mentioned in

Scripture: Solomon's, which was destroyed by the Babylonians about 587 B.C. (2 Kings 25:8,9); Zerubbabel's (Ezra 5:2; 6:15-18), and Herod's started in 20 B.C. and completed in A.D. 64. Herod's temple was destroyed in A.D. 70. The Dome of the Rock, sacred to Moslems, now stands on this site.

Men used to have to make pilgrimages to the Temple to meet God. But now we know that our bodies are the temples of God (1 Cor. 6:19). Is your body a real temple? God wishes to live in you, but He cannot if you are defiled with sin.

Read 1 Kings 9:1-28; 10:14-29 to find the possible dangers to Solomon in all his wonderful glory. Note his high position, his great wisdom, his countless riches. It is hard not to forget God in the hour of such prosperity. It was this very glory that led to Solomon's downfall.

Solomon's reputation probably spread through the voyages of his navy (1 Kings 9:21-28). The fame of Solomon was associated with Jehovah. The Queen of Sheba witnessed Solomon's reign at its zenith and was impressed by Solomon and his wisdom and wealth (1 Kings 10:1,7), his servants (v. 8), and his God (v. 9).

THE KINGDOM TORN ASUNDER
1 Kings 11,12

Solomon reigned 40 years, the second great period of the complete kingdom. At first all went well, but later there was serious trouble.

Solomon set up a great establishment in Jerusalem, built his famous Temple, and then built himself a palace that dazzled his own subjects and his foreign visitors. A rise to such prosperity and power had its dangers. It cost money and meant increased taxation. Taxes under Solomon's reign weighed the people down. Luxury and idolatry broke down their morale. During this time there was corruption and graft, and under all these burdens the people grew restless and rebellious.

For years there had been jealousy between the northern tribes and the southern tribes due mainly to the jealousy between the tribes of Ephraim and Judah. Note the blessings that Jacob gave to Ephraim (Gen. 48:17-22; 49:22-26). From the time of Joshua, who was of Ephraim's tribe, Ephraim took a leading place. The transfer of authority to Judah came under David, who was of Judah's tribe. The tribal jealousy was intensified by the hardships felt by the people through Solomon's high-handed actions. His demands created oppression and his unfaithfulness to God demanded judgment (1 Kings 11:26-43; 12:4).

A new name of great importance appears in the pages of this story: Jeroboam. This young man, of low origin, had risen to notice because of his faithful service. The prophet Ahijah made a startling revelation to Jeroboam. Using Oriental imagery, he took off his new coat, tore it into twelve strips, and said to Jeroboam, *Take for yourself ten pieces; for thus says the Lord, the God of Israel, "Behold, I will tear the kingdom out of the hand of Solomon and give you ten tribes"* (1 Kings 11:31).

When the next king, Solomon's son Rehoboam, threatened to levy heavier burdens upon the people, his headstrong action added fuel to a fire which had been burning for nearly 300 years. The revolt of the ten tribes immediately followed (1 Kings 12:16), and Jeroboam became king of the northern section (v. 20), though the two tribes of Judah and Benjamin remained loyal to Rehoboam.

The kingdom was divided. The judgment was upon Solomon for his unfaithfulness to God. Have we not seen, in our day, men of great wealth and power stripped to nothing and fleeing from outraged justice?

Things do not happen by accident. There is a cause at the root of every revolution. Religious apostasy had been gnawing like a deadly worm at the root of Israel's life. One day the tree fell. Nothing destroys a nation's life like religious decline. Take the sun out of the sky and there will be no grass, or flowers, or orchards. Take God out of our sky and there will be no homes, or schools, or social life.

THE CORRUPTION OF ISRAEL
1 Kings 12—2 Kings 17

Jeroboam, the ruler of the Northern Kingdom, Israel, made Shechem his capital. It seemed the natural place because it was in the center of the land.

It was the custom, according to the law, to go to Jerusalem regularly to worship (Deut. 12:11,14; 16:6,15,16; 1 Sam. 1:3,7). Jeroboam was afraid to have his people journey to Jerusalem, the capital of Rehoboam's kingdom, to worship God. So he made two golden calves and placed them in convenient spots (Bethel and Dan) so the people would not have to go to Jerusalem.

Over 20 times he is described as *Jeroboam, the son of Nebat, who made Israel to sin.* Beware of man-made religion. We must worship where and how God tells us! God knows we need fellowship in worship to keep the spiritual coals alive (Heb. 10:25), but we hear people say constantly that they can worship better alone in the woods or by the sea. Learn now to do what God asks you to do.

The Ministry of Elijah and Elisha

All of the kings of Israel were wicked and did not worship God, but Ahab was the worst. Elijah was a bolt of lightning that God let loose upon wicked Ahab and idolatrous Israel. *Elijah the Tishbite, who was of the settlers of Gilead,* is his brief biography. His name Elijah means "Jehovah is my God." It fitted him perfectly. He was a striking character from the highlands of Gilead. His long thick hair hung over a cloak of sheepskin. Jehovah sent him to do away with the awful worship of Baal during the reign of Ahab who had married the wicked heathen princess, Jezebel. Elijah was given power to shut up the heavens so there would be no rain for three and a half years. He called down fire from heaven before the prophets of Baal at Mount Carmel. He was the evangelist of his day, thundering out warnings to this idolatrous people. The events in this great career will intrigue you. Read them over.

Elijah trained Elisha as his successor. Elisha's ministry lasted fifty years. Most of his miracles were deeds of kindness and mercy. Elisha had a great influence upon the kings of the day and although he did not approve of what they did, he was always coming to their rescue. Elijah and Elisha are in marked contrast to one another. Elijah was the prophet of judgment, law, severity; Elisha was the prophet of grace,

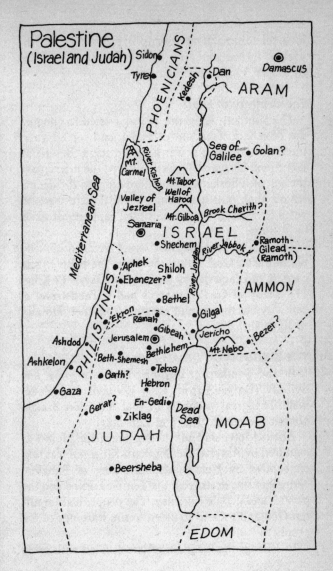

Palestine
(Israel and Judah)

Sidon
Tyre
Dan
Damascus
PHOENICIANS
ARAM
Kedesh

Sea of Galilee
Golan?

Mt. Carmel
River Kishon

Mt. Tabor
Well of Harod
Valley of Jezreel
Mt. Gilboa
Brook Cherith?

Mediterranean Sea

Samaria
ISRAEL
Shechem
River Jabbok
Ramoth-Gilead (Ramoth)

Aphek
Shiloh
Ebenezer?
AMMON

Bethel

PHILISTINES
Ekron
Raman
Gibeah
Gilgal
Jericho
Bezer?

Ashdod
Jerusalem
Bethlehem
Mt. Nebo

Ashkelon
Beth-Shemesh
Tekoa
Gath?
Hebron
Gaza
En-Gedi
Dead Sea
MOAB
Gerar?
Ziklag

JUDAH

Beersheba

EDOM

love, tenderness. Baal worship was introduced by the
wicked Jezebel and after 30 years was exterminated
by Elijah, Elisha and Jehu.

The Captivity of Israel

The Southern Kingdom of Judah tried to conquer
the Northern Kingdom of Israel, and for 80 years
there was continuous war between them. But Judah
failed, and 80 years of peace followed the marriage of
the son of Jehoshaphat (southern king) to the daughter of Ahab (northern king). Finally there were 50
years of intermittent war until the captivity of Israel
by Assyria.

The people and kings of Israel were continually
unfaithful to God. After 256 years the people were
carried into captivity by the king of Assyria (2 Kings
17). Many of God's prophets had warned Israel of
captivity but they would not turn from their idolatry
to Jehovah.

THE KINGDOM OF JUDAH 2 Kings 13—25

In the Southern Kingdom there was only one
dynasty (Davidic) from King Rehoboam to Zedekiah. The great prophets of that day were Isaiah,
Nathan, Jeremiah, Joel and Zephaniah.

About 136 years after the Northern Kingdom was
captured by Assyria, the Southern Kingdom was tak-
en captive by Nebuchadnezzar, king of Babylon.
Jerusalem was destroyed, the Temple burned and the
princes and people led away. The people had forgotten God and refused to listen to the warnings of the
prophets.

In 1 Kings the kingdom of Israel, filled with pride

and arrogance, fell apart. In 2 Kings, sinning yet more, Israel went into captivity. Surely the way of the transgressor is hard. The history of the Jews is a record of God's dealing with disobedient children. However, in all His punishment He is kind and merciful for He loves them still.

The secret of the downfall of the Jewish people is found in 2 Kings 3:2. Be loyal and true to God. It does not pay to do evil.

NOTE: There is a great difference between the fall of Israel and Judah. Israel was scattered throughout the nations for an indefinite period, but God specified the length of Judah's captivity to be 70 years. Judah was to return to Jerusalem, and she did. God used even the rulers of foreign nations to work out His plan. Cyrus, king of Persia, for example, issued a decree which allowed the Jews to return to their homeland, Palestine. The Messiah was to come out of Judah, and God prepared the way for Him to be born in Israel and not Babylon or Assyria.

1 and 2 Chronicles

Chronicles tells the history of Judah from Adam through the return from Babylonian captivity. It is through such books as the Chronicles that we get the history of the Jewish nation. Through this nation our Lord came to earth. God chose this people for the fulfillment of His great promises and purposes. He is still their God (Rom. 11:1), and He has His purposes yet to be fulfilled in them. In the light of this truth, books such as the Chronicles take on new meaning and power.

In reading 2 Chronicles, notice the great revivals under Asa (2 Chron. 15), Jehoshaphat (2 Chron. 20), Joash (2 Chron. 23; 24), Hezekiah (2 Chron. 29—31).

Minimum Daily Requirements/Spiritual Vitamins

Sunday: Building and dedicating the Temple (1 Kings 6:1-14; 8:22-53)

Monday: Solomon's glorious reign (1 Kings 10:1-29)

Tuesday: The kingdom divided (1 Kings 12:1-33)

Wednesday: The prophet Elijah (1 Kings 17:1—18:46)

Thursday: Elijah and Elisha (2 Kings 2:1-22)

Friday: The captivity of Israel—The Northern Kingdom (2 Kings 17:7-23)

Saturday: The captivity of Judah—The Southern Kingdom (2 Kings 25:1-21)

Return of the Remnant
(Ezra and Nehemiah)

12

Ezra and Nehemiah tell the story of one of the most important events in Jewish history—the return of God's chosen people from exile in Babylon. The Old Testament history closes about 100 years after the Jews returned from their captivity.

RETURN AND REBUILDING Ezra 1—6

Cyrus, king of Persia, permitted the Jews who were captives in his kingdom to return to Jerusalem (Ezra 1:1-6). Two hundred years before, Isaiah had prophesied that God would do this. He even named Cyrus as the one God would use (Isa. 44:28; 45:1-4).

At Cyrus' first call in 537 B.C. (Ezra 1:1-4) no more than 50,000 Jews returned to Jerusalem under Zerubbabel. Their names are given in chapter 2. Not everyone returned. After 70 years, most of them had built homes and established themselves and were content to remain in Babylon.

Everything is taken care of when God is in charge. Money for rebuilding the Temple in Jerusalem, trav-

eling expenses and all other needs were provided by
God through Cyrus (1:4,6). Cyrus also gave back to
Zerubbabel the golden vessels which Nebuchadnezzar had taken from the Temple in Jerusalem (1:5-11).
Then the Jews started back over 700 miles of track-
less desert from Babylon to Jerusalem. (From this
time the Israelites are called Jews because most of
them were of the tribe of Judah and the name Jews
comes from Judah.)

Upon returning they did not build the Temple first,
but the altar (3:2). The place where sin is dealt with
must come first in every life. The heart must be right
if God is to bless. The altar was the center of the Jew's
religion as the cross is the center of the Christian
faith.

Then they laid the foundation of the Temple. It was
a time of great rejoicing. Read about the hindrances
to finishing the Temple (4:1-22). Hindrances to all
real work for God are to be expected. The opposition
disheartened them. But Haggai and Zechariah, the
prophets, encouraged the people (4:23—5:17). Within four years the Temple was complete and dedicated
(Ezra 6).

Zerubbabel's Temple was very plain and simple. It
was not the sumptuous edifice that Solomon's was. In
fact, it was in such contrast to the elegance of the first
Temple that the old men who had seen Solomon's
Temple wept aloud. But it was God's house and so
the people thanked God and took courage.

RETURN AND REFORMATION UNDER EZRA
Ezra 7—10

At least 60 years after the Jews had first returned

to Jerusalem Ezra led a second expedition from Babylon to Israel (458 B.C.). Ezra received a commission from Artaxerxes, the king, (7:11—8:14) who aided in accomplishing God's plans for His people. Read Ezra 7:25 and learn how impressed the king was with Ezra's love of God's Word. Oh, that we might live in such a way that others would learn to have respect for God's Book!

This contingent under Ezra consisted of 1700 Jews. It took them four months to make the journey, and it was financed by King Artaxerxes (7:12-26). Thirteen years later this same king authorized Nehemiah to build the walls of Jerusalem (Neh. 2). Cyrus, Darius and Artaxerxes, the three Persian kings, were very friendly to the Jews.

Tradition tells us that Ezra was the founder of the synagogue worship which arose during the captivity. Because the Temple had been destroyed and the people were scattered, they needed some place to worship God. Each Jewish community had its place of worship and instruction, or synagogue.

Ezra wrote and worked to keep the record intact, and to hold Israel to her divinely appointed mission. We are indebted to Ezra for the literary and ecclesiastical renaissance of that day.

In addition to Ezra's outstanding ministry of the Word, he probably wrote Psalm 119 and portions of 1 and 2 Chronicles. Assisted by the Great Synagogue of which he was president, he settled the canon of Old Testament Scripture. Under Ezra a great revival of Bible study took place.

When Ezra returned to Jerusalem, he found things even worse than he had expected. Although the people had not returned to idolatry, they had inter-married with the people of the land and had done things the heathen had taught them (Ezra 9:1-4). The princes and rulers were the worst offenders. Ezra tore his garments and pulled out his hair in grief! Read Ezra's touching prayer and confession (9:5-15).

As Ezra was praying and weeping before God, a great congregation assembled. What happened? Read 10:1-44. The people who had gathered about him came to a consciousness of the greatness of their sin when they saw how it affected Ezra. Finally one of their number spoke and acknowledged the sin. At once Ezra led them into a sacred covenant with God. Turn now to Nehemiah 9:5-38 and you will find the prayer of Nehemiah. Nehemiah's prayer began where Ezra's ended—with utter surrender to God. Compare Nehemiah 9:1,2 with Ezra 9:15; 10:1.

God promised to bring the Jews back after 70 years in Babylon (Jer. 25:11,12; 29:10). The restoration was wholly undeserved by Israel. It was an act of God's mercy. See the results of this restoration of God's people to their land. First, through the rebuilding of the Temple, God opened the door of fellowship with Himself. Second, He renewed His promise of a coming Redeemer. It was prophesied that the Redeemer would be associated with the land of Israel. Third, He made ready for the *fullness of the time* when Christ should come (Gal. 4:4).

NEHEMIAH'S LEADERSHIP

Nehemiah was the cupbearer at the court of King Artaxerxes—a position of high honor. Yet he had not forgotten his people. The news that was brought to him about Jerusalem made him very sad, and the king detected this sadness. The Jews had been back home for 100 years, but had made no attempt to build Jerusalem beyond the restoration of the Temple.

Artaxerxes' stepmother was Esther, the Jewish queen who no doubt was still alive. Nehemiah may have received his appointment through her influence. He was loyal enough to his people to leave the luxury of a king's court and go back to rebuild Jerusalem. The king gave consent.

When Nehemiah reached Jerusalem in 445 B.C., Ezra had been there for 13 years. Ezra was a priest and had been teaching the people the Word of God. But Nehemiah was a civil governor. He had come with the authority of the king of Persia to build the walls of Jerusalem. After he had been there only three days, he went up and viewed the walls at night. When he saw their dilapidated condition, he encouraged the people to begin building immediately. In spite of problems, the work was accomplished in 52 days by assigning a portion of the wall to each family!

First, the enemies of the Jews derided them. They hindered their work so that the Jews had to keep watch night and day. Their derision turned to anger and Nehemiah divided the men into two groups, one keeping watch while the other worked.

Then some of the Jews became tired and complained that there was so much rubbish that the walls could not be built. The enemies also tried by craft to bring Nehemiah away from his building, but Nehemiah prayed and again he foiled his enemy.

When finished, Nehemiah gave the city of Jerusalem into the charge of his brother Hanani (Neh. 7:1-4). When he took a census (7:5-73) the number was more than 49,000. All the people gathered together and requested Ezra, the scribe, to bring out the book of the Law of Moses. When he read and explained the Law to the people (Neh. 8:1-13), this public reading brought true repentance and revival to the people.

Captivity in Babylon cured the Jews of idolatry. Up to that time, in spite of all the warnings of the prophets, the people worshiped the idols of the peoples around them. But from the days of the captivity to the present the Jews have never been guilty of this sin.

Minimum Daily Requirements/Spiritual Vitamins
Sunday: Jews return to Jerusalem (Ezra 1—3)
Monday: Discouragement and joy (Ezra 4—6)
Tuesday: Ezra's expedition (Ezra 7—10)
Wednesday: Nehemiah rebuilds the wall (Neh. 1—3)
Thursday: Overcoming opposition (Neh. 4—6)
Friday: Nehemiah rebuilds the morals (Neh. 7—9)
Saturday: Reforming through religion (Neh. 11—13)

The Court Intrigues
of Esther

13

The great Xerxes, king of Persia, was also Ahasuerus of the Book of Esther. Historians tell us that his famous expedition against Greece, when the Greeks defeated his fleet at the battle of Salamis in 480 B.C. was one of the world's most important battles. From Herodotus we find that the feast described in the first chapter of Esther was the occasion for planning the campaign against Greece (third year of Xerxes' reign). Esther replaced Vashti in the seventh year of his reign (Esther 2:16).

Although God's name is not mentioned in the Book of Esther, every page is full of God, who hides Himself behind every word. Matthew Henry, the great Bible commentator, says, "If the name of God is not here, His finger is."

The Book of Esther opens with a feast of the world's prince—Ahasuerus; it closes with the feast of God's prince—Mordecai. In point of time, the events of Esther occurred between chapters 6 and 7 of the Book of Ezra.

VASHTI AND ESTHER Esther 1,2

As the book of Esther opens the king was entertaining all the nobles and princes of his kingdom in the royal palace at Shushan. The men were feasting in the palace gardens and the women were entertained by Queen Vashti in her private apartment.

When the king and princes were in the midst of their drunken revelry, the king called for Vashti so he could show off her beauty. No Persian woman would permit this; drunkenness had outraged the most sacred rules of Oriental etiquette. Vashti refused. This made the king a laughingstock, so he deposed the queen (see Esther 1:12-22).

Between chapters 1 and 2 of Esther, Ahasuerus made his historic attack on Greece with an army of 5,000,000 men and suffered a terrible defeat. Two years later he married Esther and she was his queen for 13 years. She no doubt lived into the reign of her stepson Artaxerxes and it was her influence at court that made it possible for Nehemiah to rebuild Jerusalem under Artaxerxes (see Neh. 2:1-8).

PLOTTING OF HAMAN Esther 3,4

In Esther 3 begins the story of Haman, a wicked man whose day of triumph was short and whose joy endured but for a moment. He was a wicked monster in the life of God's chosen people.

Haman was exalted to the highest position under the king of Persia (3:1). He swelled with vanity and was bitterly humiliated when Mordecai, the porter at the gate, did not do homage to him as to the king (3:2). Mordecai, a Jew, could not give divine honor to a man! Haman became so enraged that he wanted to have a wholesale massacre of all the Jews in the kingdom (3:6). Haman told the king that a certain nation of people were disloyal subjects and offered to pay the king a bribe if he would allow them to be killed. The king signed a royal decree that they should be killed and all their property taken.

Imagine the fasting and praying and the weeping in sackcloth that took place among the Jews (4:1-3). Queen Esther saw it all and inquired of Mordecai what it meant. He gave her a copy of the king's decree and asked her to plead with the king for mercy. Then he added, *And who knows whether you have not attained royalty for such a time as this?* (4:14).

It would do well for each one of us to pause and ask himself this same question. Why has God allowed me to live at this particular hour? To do what is right may mean that we must jeopardize our lives. Then we must face the issue and answer with this young queen, *And if I perish, I perish* (4:16).

DELIVERANCE OF THE JEWS Esther 5—10

Queen Esther answered the challenge of Mordecai. She acted at terrible danger to herself for the sake of her people, the Jews. Read Esther 5. It was a daring act for her to enter unsummoned into the presence of the king. Who could tell what this fickle monarch would do? Think what he had done to Queen Vashti!

When Esther was received by the king, she used her resources. She knew the king's weakness for good living so she invited him to a banquet. Read what happened that night when the king could not sleep (Esther 6:1-11). How was Haman trapped? (Esther

6:6). At the second banquet Esther pleaded for her own life. She had Haman on the spot. The king granted Esther's wish.

Read Esther 7:7-10. Haman was hanged on the very scaffold he had prepared for Mordecai, and Mordecai was elevated to the place of honor next to the king.

The Book of Esther closes with the account of the establishment of the Feast of Purim. It was to be celebrated annually to mark the deliverance of the Jews from a fearful danger. It was a Thanksgiving Day for the chosen people. Although they had forsaken God, He had spared them. Deliverance seems to be the keynote of Jewish history.

This Book of Esther is an important link in a chain of events that tell of the re-establishment of the Hebrew nation in their own land in preparation for the coming of the Messiah into the world. The Jews had escaped extermination. It was God's purpose that they should be preserved to bring forth the Saviour of the world.

Minimum Daily Requirements/Spiritual Vitamins
Sunday: Rejection of Vashti (Esther 1)
Monday: Crowning of Esther (Esther 2)
Tuesday: Plotting of Haman (Esther 3; 4)
Wednesday: Venture of Esther (Esther 5)
Thursday: Mordecai exalted (Esther 6)
Friday: Esther's feast (Esther 7; 8)
Saturday: Deliverance of the Jews (Esther 9,10)

Suffering of a Righteous Man (Job)

14

We have finished reading the historical books of the Old Testament—Joshua through Esther. Now we open the books of poetry—Job, Psalms, Proverbs, Ecclesiastes and Song of Solomon. These books tell of the experiences of the heart.

Job's key word is "tried" (Job 23:10). Trials and suffering are not always for our punishment but sometimes for our education and training. The athlete is not put under strict discipline for punishment but merely to make him ready for the race. Christ is ever preparing us for the race that is set before us (see Heb. 12:1,2).

Tennyson called Job "the greatest poem, whether of ancient or modern literature." It is set in the patriarchal days. This book may be one of the most ancient pieces of finished literature in existence. It is one of the oldest books, if not the oldest, in the Bible. The Word of God settles the fact that Job was a real person (Ezek. 14:14,20).

It is fitting that the oldest book should deal with the oldest problems. Among these is, "Why do godly people suffer?" People have always asked why God permits good people to suffer.

SATAN AND THE SAINT Job 1:6—2:10

In Job 1:6 the "sons of God" presented themselves before the King. The "sons of God" are angelic beings, the messengers of God. The mystery is that Satan was among them. He was angelic, but he had fallen. There was no hint that he was out of place.

In contrast to the Almighty we have the adversary Satan. He is depicted as a real being, not an imaginary one. We cannot help but contrast the Satan of the Book of Job with the grotesque figure depicted by the poets. The Bible tells us that Satan comes as *an angel of light* to deceive and to tempt (2 Cor. 11:14).

Satan has great power, but there are limits to his might. Satan is mighty, but God is Almighty! Satan can break through only where God allows (Job 1:10, 12). No calamity can come to us that the Father does not allow (Job 38:8,11). God will never let us be tempted above our endurance (see 1 Cor. 10:13).

Satan claims that Job only serves God for what he can get out of it. Job is not so much on trial here as God. It is not a question of Job's loyalty so much as it is one of God's power. Even today some say that ministers are preaching the gospel for what they can get out of it; that some people turn to Christ only to gain food and shelter.

So God says, "All right, try it out! Take everything away from Job and see what happens!" The real conflict here was between God and Satan. God was proving the truth about Job's integrity in following Him.

When the trials came and Job lost his children, wealth and health, Job did not understand the meaning of all his suffering. He knew it was not because he had sinned, as his friends said. He wondered what God was doing. We will not always understand what God is working out on the battleground of our hearts, but there is a reason and value for everything that God allows (Rom. 8:28). Man will never find the answer to all of God's dealings. Men may be honest and sincere as far as they go in trying to explain things, as were Job's friends, but some of God's ways are past finding out.

Do not be surprised to find problems in every congregation of God's children. Satan comes to do mischief to saints. He distracts our attention. He sets us to criticizing. He sows dissension in the congregation. He excites the pride of preachers and singers. He chills our spirit and freezes our prayers. Yes, when the Word is being sown, the fowls of the air come to pluck it away (Matt. 13:3-23). You can never walk before God and try to lead a godly life without Satan coming in to walk with you—accusing you, finding fault and vexing you.

JOB AND HIS FRIENDS Job 2:11—37:24

Get acquainted with Job's friends: courtly Eliphaz, argumentative Bildad, blunt Zophar, and the youthful Elihu. There are things we can say in favor of these men although their words of "comfort" were anything but that. They came to Job. They were friends who stuck through adversity. When all the multitude of acquaintances had forgotten Job, they came. They

113

also kept still for seven days. This is good! They seemed to be trying to find out the reason for all of Job's troubles before they spoke. Someone has said that instead of talking about Job, they came and talked with him.

They all had an explanation for why Job was suffering as he was—Job must have sinned miserably to have caused this suffering. Eliphaz backs his argument by a dream (Job. 4:1—5:27); Bildad, by some old proverbs (chap. 8); Zophar, by experience and reason (chap. 11). Elihu came nearest the truth when he argued that suffering was God's discipline to bring the soul back into fellowship with God; but it was not the whole truth.

God called Job *blameless and upright* (1:8). His friends were wrong in charging that sin was the only possible cause of his calamities.

WRETCHED COMFORTERS

The chief question returns: "Why does God permit the righteous to suffer?" Job cried out, "I cannot understand it. It doesn't seem right."

Job's wife, looking on discouraged, says, "Something is wrong. Your religion is a failure. Curse God and die." This is the voice of despair.

Eliphaz adds, "God never makes a mistake. What have you done to bring this on yourself?"

Bildad says, "God is just. Confess your sin."

Zophar says next, "God is all-wise. He knows man."

Elihu, God's man, says the wisest thing, "God is good; look up, and trust Him, for He is God."

Then Jehovah speaks from the whirlwind (Job 40: 7). The scene begins with God gloriously revealing Himself. In a series of questions God says, in effect, "Who can do all these things but myself?" God is thus revealed to Job, and Job to himself.

As so often is true with us, when Job came into the presence of God, he forgot the speech he thought he would make! (40:4,5). There was no arguing with God. Job went down on his face, repenting *in dust and ashes* (42:1-6). This is the only place to learn God's lesson—on your face with your mouth shut!

When we bow to God's will, we find God's way. Stoop to conquer. Bend to obey. This is the lesson of Job. This is the victory of submissive faith.

Jehovah explains to Job (by revealing Himself to him) that when men see God something always happens. The godly are allowed to suffer that they may see themselves. When Isaiah saw himself as he really was, he fell on his face and cried out, *I am a man of unclean lips* (Isa. 6:5).

Did you ever think that you looked all right until a friend dropped in to invite you to go some place with him? When you saw how immaculate your friend looked, you immediately realized how you needed to clean up. So often this is true in the presence of Christ. The very perfection of His Person makes us feel sinful. Measure your life by His life and you will feel as Job did.

God allows His children to suffer in order to reveal character, to set forth an object lesson, and to bring to light some hidden sin. In Job's case, that hidden sin was self-righteousness.

At the end, Job enjoyed a double portion of prosperity from the hand of God. This book well illustrates Romans 8:28. How wonderful to hear of the patience of Job and to see the Lord's pity and mercy. A morning of joy always follows the night of sorrow.

Job found God in his trouble. Many know God as a Creator and believe in His greatness, but they do not really know God. The more we understand His ways the more we will love Him and put our trust in Him.

Be sure to read the following references: Job 1:21; 5:17; 13:15; 14:14; 16:21; 19:23-27; 23:10; 26:7-14; 28:12-28; 42:1-6. These are some of the most frequently quoted and best loved passages in the Bible.

Minimum Daily Requirements/Spiritual Vitamins
Sunday: Satan and saint (Job 1:1,2—2:13)
Monday: Bildad thinks Job a hypocrite (Job 8:1-22)
Tuesday: Job answers his friends (Job 12:1-25)
Wednesday: Job's faith (Job 19:1-29)
Thursday: Job and Elihu (Job 32:1-22; 37:23,24)
Friday: God speaks to Job (Job 38:1-18)
Saturday: Job vindicated and honored (Job 42:1-17)

Praising God with Psalms

No doubt Psalms is the best loved book in the Old Testament. Someone has called it the solid gold of Christian experience. Slip in wherever you will and you will find a treasure. Every psalm is a direct expression of the soul's consciousness of God. With which psalms are you familiar?

The Psalms is the national hymnbook of Israel. It contains 150 poems to be set to music for worship. Worship is the central idea. The Psalms magnify and praise the Lord, exalt His attributes, His names, His word and His goodness. Every human experience is related to Him. The life of the believer is pictured in all of its experiences of joy and sorrow, victory and failure.

The Psalms are full of Christ and describe His suffering and death:

His prophetic office is found in Psalm 22:22;
His priestly office in Psalms 40:6,8; 22; 110;
His kingly office in Psalms 2; 21; 45; 72;
His sufferings in Psalms 22 and 69;

117

His resurrection in Psalm 16.

Another useful classification of the Psalms may be made according to the subjects:

Instruction 1; 19

Praise 8; 29; 93; 100

Thanksgiving 30; 65; 103; 107; 116

Penitence 6; 32; 38; 51; 102; 130; 143

Trust 3; 27; 31; 46; 56; 62; 86

Distress 4; 13; 55; 64; 88

Aspiration 42; 63; 84; 137

History 78; 105; 106

Prophecy (psalms of the Messiah) 2; 16; 22; 24; 40; 45; 68; 69; 72; 97; 110; 118

There are also numerous quotations from this book found in the New Testament.

We speak of the Psalms as the Psalms of David. He has been considered the principal writer. Of the 150 psalms, 73 are assigned to him and 50 are anonymous. Psalm 90 is by Moses. Two are by Solomon— Psalms 72 and 127. Asaph (David's choir leader), the sons of Korah (a family of official musicians) and Jeduthun also wrote some. But let us not be too engrossed in finding who penned them. Let us rather read and enjoy these grand expressions of praise. They are of God for you.

MAN, HIS BLESSEDNESS, FALL AND RECOVERY
Psalms 1—41

1. Man blessed .... Psalm 1
2. Man fallen from his high position and at enmity with God .... Psalms 2 and 14
3. Man restored by his blessed Redeemer, the Man Christ Jesus .... Psalms 16—41

In this section we have a collection of the psalms which David wrote. Psalm 1 tells of the road to success. List the things it says to do, things not to do and the results of following each list.

Some psalms in this group that show the final blessings of man because of the glorious work of Christ Jesus are Psalms 22; 23; 24. Psalm 22 tells of the Good Shepherd giving His life for His sheep. We see the cross and hear the cries of our dying Saviour. As you read this psalm, you will recognize the facts. Psalm 23 tells of the great Shepherd keeping His sheep. He promises to guide and provide and keep His people. Psalm 24 tells of the chief Shepherd in His glory rewarding His sheep. He is my King and He is coming to reign in power and great glory.

In Psalm 22 we see the crucifixion of Christ portrayed here more clearly than in any other part of the Old Testament. Read and compare these verses.

Psalm 22:1 .... Matthew 27:46
Psalm 22:6,7 .... Luke 23:35,36
Psalm 22:6-8 .... Matthew 27:39,41,43
Psalm 22:12,13 .... Matthew 27:36,44
Psalm 22:28 .... 1 Corinthians 15:23,24

ISRAEL Psalms 42—72
1. Her ruin .... Psalms 42—49
2. Her redeemer .... Psalms 50—60
3. Her redemption .... Psalms 61—72

This section opens with "a cry" from the depth of oppression (see Psalms 42—49). It ends with the King reigning over the redeemed nation in Psalm 72. Read this glorious psalm.

There are several psalms of penitence, but the chief

is Psalm 51. Second Samuel 11 and 12 tell the story of David's sin. When you read this, notice three things that are said. When Nathan the prophet told David the story of the despicable fellow who took the only lamb belonging to the poor man, and said to David: *You are the man!* David did not try to dodge the issue but said, *I have sinned against the Lord.* Then Nathan reassured him, saying, *The Lord also has taken away your sin* (2 Sam. 12:13).

Notice in Psalm 51 these words, *Against Thee, Thee only, I have sinned, and done what is evil in Thy sight.* This psalm is a prayer of contrition and confession. David cries for mercy from a God whom he knows is merciful and full of loving-kindness. We too must confess our sin to God and remember that God forgives (1 John 1:9). Whenever a man is sincere in his confession to God, He will cleanse his sin.

THE SANCTUARY Psalms 73—89

In this third section the sanctuary is mentioned or referred to in almost every psalm. They are concerned almost entirely with material used in worship and need little comment. The sanctuary is seen from its ruin to its restoration in the fullness of blessing.

THE EARTH Psalms 90—106

Blessing needed .... Psalms 90—94
Blessing anticipated .... Psalms 95—100
Blessing enjoyed............... Psalms 101—106

The first of this group of psalms was written during the wanderings in the wilderness. The psalms are not arranged in chronological order.

Read the opening verses of Psalms 90 and 91 together. If God is our dwelling place on this earth, we shall live in confidence, sheltered by the Almighty. Read what Christ says in John 15:7. The secret of a godly life is abiding in the Almighty. We are told that there is a point of perfect calm at the center of a hurricane. There may be raging stormy snares, pestilences, darkness and destruction, but when the soul is abiding under the shadow of the Almighty, it is safe.

If you wish to praise the Lord for His goodness, read Psalm 103. Its worship, adoration, praise and thanksgiving is great exercise for the soul.

THE WORD OF GOD Psalms 107—150

The teaching in these psalms centers around the Word of God. Psalm 107 gives the key: *He sent His word and healed them* (v. 20).

Psalm 119 is the greatest psalm of the whole book. It extols the Word of God which is the great revelation of the heart and mind of the Lord. Almost every verse speaks of God's word, or law, or precepts or statutes.

PSALMS AND PRAISE

Man's chief end is to glorify God. There is no heaven either here or in the world to come for people who do not praise God. If you do not enter into the spirit and worship of heaven, the spirit and joy of heaven cannot enter you! Probably no other book has so largely influenced men's lives, given expression to their deepest experiences, and woven itself into the very fiber of their character as the Book of Psalms.

This book is used by Hebrew and Christian alike

even in our day. The Psalms were for use in the Temple, for which many were prepared. They were written for the heart to worship God out under the open heavens or in the pit of despair, or in a cave of hiding. When you find yourself in deep need, you can always find a psalm which expresses your inmost feeling. Or, if you have an abounding joy, the words are there for you, too.

It is the book for all who are in need, the sick and suffering, the poor and needy, the prisoner and exile, the man in danger, the persecuted. It is a book for the sinner, telling him of God's great mercy and forgiveness. It is a book for the child of God, leading him into new experiences with the Lord. It tells of God's law in its perfection and pronounces blessings upon the one who will keep it.

The Psalms begin with the word "blessed" and there is not one "woe" in the entire Psalms.

Minimum Daily Requirements/Spiritual Vitamins
Sunday: Psalms of law (Pss. 1,19)
Monday: Psalms of creation (Pss. 29,104)
Tuesday: Psalms of judgment (Pss. 52,53)
Wednesday: Psalms of Christ (Pss. 22; 40; 41)
Thursday: Psalms of life (Pss. 3,31)
Friday: Psalms of the heart (Pss. 37,42)
Saturday: Psalms of God (Pss. 90,139)

Jesus Christ, Our Wisdom;
the End of All Living;
the Lover of Our Souls

The Wisdom of Proverbs, Ecclesiastes and Song of Solomon

16

Notice how the Book of Proverbs opens—*The proverbs of Solomon.* Solomon was a great king, famous for his wisdom and riches. Our duty to God, to neighbors, the duty of parents and children, our obligations as citizens are set forth in Proverbs. Every relationship in life is mentioned.

The real power and beauty in this book lies in the true meaning of the word "wisdom." This word means more than an excellent attribute. It is found that the wisdom of Proverbs is the Incarnate Word of the New Testament. Wisdom is represented as dwelling with God from all eternity. Compare Proverbs 8:23-31 with John 1:1,2; Hebrews 1:2 and Colossians 2:3. When you read the Book of Proverbs put Christ instead of wisdom in the verse (see 1 Cor. 1:30). You will see a wonderful power in this book (1 John 5:20).

The purpose of the Book of Proverbs is stated clearly at the beginning. Read Proverbs 1:2-4. The first of all duties is the fear of God (Prov. 1:7).

"Worship God"—It's the first step to wisdom (1:7).

"Walk Straight!"—The "straight and narrow" has the lowest accident rate (2:20).

"Directions"—Ask God about everything (3:6).

"Watch Your Step!"—Every step helps mold character; step well (4:26).

"Flee Flattery"—Don't be manipulated (5:3).

"God's Black List"—Avoid pride, lies, murder, deceit, mischief, betrayal, discord (6:17-19).

"A Bad Woman"—Read carefully Proverbs 7:15-27.

"Riches"—Rubies of wisdom command highest prices on the market of character values (8:11).

"More Fun"—Nothing you ought not to do is ever "more fun." Wait till you see what results (9:17,18).

"Silence"—Wordy men seldom are wise men (10:19).

This whole book is extremely practical. Study it closely for guidance in daily life.

The fear of the Lord spoken of here is not fright but the fear of a son who does not want to grieve his father's love. It is this fear coming from love, the fear of displeasing God, that leads to godliness.

The duty of parents to chastise their children is enforced, and is based upon God's chastening of His children (3:11,12). One of the signs of the last wicked days upon the earth is given by Paul as "disobedience to parents" (see 2 Tim. 3:2).

The young are warned against the influence of bad

124

companions, impurity, intemperance, anger, strife, and quarrels (Prov. 1:10-19; 4:14-19; 19; and chapters 3; 10; 13; 15; 16; 18).

There are many sins of the tongue. We use it too freely. We lie and are deceitful in dealings with others. Guard the tongue, for in the tongue is the power of life and death (12:22; 18:21).

Read about pride and its consequences in Proverbs 8; 11; 16; 19. See Proverbs 16:18. The Lord wants us to be humble before Him and not think we are better than others. Every truly great person is humble.

The author is pleading with us to shun evil companions, pride, envy, intemperance, sins of the tongue and idleness. This would be impossible to do unless we had Christ, the Wisdom of God, within us.

Counsel for All Men Proverbs 11—20

"False Economy"—A gift is never lost; only what is selfishly kept impoverishes (11:24).

"Fools"—You cannot convince a fool of his folly; but a wise man will accept rebuke (12:15).

"Lying"—Righteousness and lying are enemies; to a wicked man they are synonymous (13:5).

"Answers that Heal"—Two people ought not to get angry at the same time (15:1).

"Clean Sin"—A man deep in wickedness will invent "pretty names for sin" (Spurgeon) (16:2).

"Drink Up!"—If you decide for strong drink don't be surprised when it decides against you (20:1).

"Self-Control"—A guarded mouth makes for a se-
rene soul (21:23).

"Reputation"—Choose a good name rather than
riches. Your name goes on; your
wealth stops at death (22:1).

"Counsel"—The sober judgment of a sane thinking
group is more reliable than your own
opinion (24:6).

"Women"—Better solitude on top of the house than
living with a nagging woman (25:24).

"Gossip"—Fire goes out when fuel gives out; scandal
stops when mouths are stopped (26:20).

"Tomorrow"—There is never a tomorrow, only today. Get it done now. Now soon
becomes then (27:1).

"Understanding"—Rank does not guarantee an
understanding heart (28:16).

"Bribes"—Seek justice and your land shall stand; accept bribes and it will fall (29:4).

"Security"—God is the only safe soul-armor (30:5).

ECCLESIASTES AND MAN'S WISDOM

Ecclesiastes is the soul's autobiography or the book
of experience. "Vanity" is the key word (Eccles. 2:
11). God has given us in the Book of Ecclesiastes the
record of all that human thinking and natural religion
has ever been able to discover concerning the meaning and goal of life. The arguments in the book are not
God's arguments, but God's record of man's arguments. This explains why some passages are at vari-
ance with the rest of the Bible.

The writer is Solomon, and the book is a dramatic autobiography of his experience and reflections while he was out of fellowship with God. Ecclesiastes has its origin in his tragic sin of forsaking God and seeking satisfaction in philosophy and science. The message of Ecclesiastes is that, apart from God, life is full of weariness and disappointment.

The great question: "Is life worth living?" is presented. Solomon tested it to the full. No man could better do it or better tell it—and the answer he gives is important for modern man.

The problem which faced Solomon was how he could find happiness and satisfaction apart from God (1:1-3). He sought satisfaction in science (1:4-11), but could get no answer. He sought it in philosophy and wisdom (1:12-18), but in vain. He found pleasure (2:1-11), mirth (v. 1), drinking (v. 3), building (v. 4), gardening (vv. 5,6), possessions (v. 7), wealth and music (v. 8), all empty. Materialism (2:12-26), fatalism (3:1-15), deism (3:1—4:16), natural religion (5:1-8), wealth (5:9—6:12), and even morality and reputation (7:1—12:12) proved equally fruitless.

Now comes a turning point. Read Ecclesiastes 8:12 and 12:13. The "Preacher," as he is called, has been looking out and back and around. Now he looks up and sees God and is satisfied. The phrase *under the sun* (1:3) is found 28 times in this little book. The "under-the-sun-life" is hardly worth living; but above the sun, and in the heavenlies that Paul describes, it is glorious (Eph. 1).

We can never find satisfaction and happiness in this world. True happiness apart from Christ is impossible. We find dissatisfaction among the poor and

127

rich alike, among the ignorant and learned, among people and kings.

Ecclesiastes closes with a call to the young! Lay the foundations early (11:9—12:1).

THE SONG OF SOLOMON

The Song of Solomon has been called the Christian's Love Song. The key text is Song of Solomon 6:3. This is a song of love in marriage using Oriental imagery. The persons are Solomon and the Shulamite maid and the daughters of Jerusalem. The idea of the love of husband and wife sets forth the love between Jehovah and His people. This is seen in many passages in the Bible. Personal love of Christ is the greatest need of the Church today. The knowledge of sin forgiven and of Christ's redeeming work has drawn us to Him.

Minimum Daily Requirements/Spiritual Vitamins
Sunday: Get wisdom (Prov. 1—4)
Monday: To sons (Prov. 5—7)
Tuesday: Good and bad (Prov. 15—17)
Wednesday: Wise words (Prov. 20; 22; 31)
Thursday: All is vanity (Eccles. 1—3)
Friday: Only God satisfies (Eccles. 11; 12)
Saturday: Love (Song of Sol. 1:1-7; 2:1-7)

Isaiah and the Coming Messiah

17

The prophets were men whom God raised up during the dark days of Israel's history. They were the evangelists of the day, the religious patriots of the hour. Read what God says about them in 2 Kings 17:13. The period of the prophets in Israel covered 500 years from the ninth to the fourth century B.C. These prophets spoke fearlessly to kings and people alike of their sins and failures. Then their voices were silenced until John the Baptist.

The prophets were the most unpopular men in their day because they dealt with the moral and religious conditions of the hour which were generally bad! Prophets were sent when the nation was out of step with God and walking in disobedience. The words the prophets used to rebuke or exhort the people were very pointed, and truth is seldom popular with the sinner.

The Assyrian captivity of Israel (the Northern Kingdom) and the Babylonian captivity of Judah (the

129

Southern Kingdom) are largely the theme of the Old Testament prophets (see 2 Kings 17:1-23; 24:11—25:21). Some prophets served before the exile and some afterwards. These are called pre-exilic and post-exilic prophets.

In the Gospels, you find the phrase *that it might be fulfilled*. We find in studying these passages that God fulfills prophecy literally. Learn to interpret the words of the prophets in a literal, natural way. Do not force a spiritual interpretation and read out all the real meaning. There are figurative passages, of course. But you will find that as soon as you determine the meaning of the figure, that, too, will have its literal fulfillment.

ISAIAH

Isaiah was a man who certainly spoke boldly to his own time, but as a prophet he spoke of the future as well; hence he is the prophet of all times. We follow his index finger as it points into the future and we hear him say, "Lo, your King!"

This great prophet of the Southern Kingdom of Judah lived at the time the Northern Kingdom of Israel was destroyed by Assyria and his voice saved Judah during these trying hours. It is interesting to note that this is also the time Rome, Sparta and Athens were founded.

The Book of Isaiah is written with two distinct emphases. In the first of the book he pictured Israel. In the last of the book, the prophet beheld Jesus bearing our load of sin; then he beheld Christ exalted and glorified and shouted of his vision from the housetop.

UNDER UZZIAH AND JOTHAM Isaiah 1—6

Isaiah was prophet during the reigns of Uzziah, Jotham, Ahaz and Hezekiah (Isa. 1:1). During this time he preached in Jerusalem and warned Judah of her folly and rebellion (1:2-9). They had separated themselves from God by the sins of greed, heathen alliances and idolatry (2:6-9). God called them a fruitless vine.

Now turn to Isaiah 6:1-13 and you see that Isaiah received his real commission the year King Uzziah (Azariah) died. No doubt he had written chapters 1—5 before this time. Uzziah's reign of 52 years that was glorious during the greater part ended in gloom. The last four years of his life Uzziah was a leper. He was shut off from the business of state, and the kingdom was ruled by his son Jotham.

Jotham, Uzziah's successor, is only mentioned twice in the book (1:1; 7:1). It is with the reign of the next two kings, Ahaz and Hezekiah, that Isaiah's prophecy deals.

UNDER AHAZ Isaiah 7—14

Read Isaiah 7:1. Ahaz was utterly bad. He was an open idolater. For this sin God allowed Rezin, king of Syria, and Pekah, king of Israel, to invade his kingdom. Isaiah had been silent under Jotham but this invasion brought him to the front in his ministry (7:3). He appealed to Ahaz to put his trust in God for help rather than call in Tiglath-Pileser from Nineveh.

God sent the prophet to encourage Ahaz. Beside predicting the Assyrian invasion in Isaiah 8, the prophet saw an end to Israel's troubles through the birth of the Christ-child who would rule over the kingdom of David in righteousness forever. He gave Ahaz a "sign" that Judah was not to perish—the prophecy of Immanuel, the virgin's Son, Jesus Christ. Read these important words in Isaiah 7:10-16. However, Ahaz pursued his own plans with Assyria. But that nation on which Judah now leaned was to become the means of punishment (7:17-20).

Then followed the sentence of doom upon king and land (8:6-22). With nations, this was God's policy: doom for idolatry.

In Isaiah 9:6,7 we find another great prophecy concerning Christ. The Son to be given, the Child to be born, was to sit on David's throne. Remember the "throne of David" is as definite as the "throne of the Caesars." Read the angel's words to Mary in Luke 1:32,33.

We find present woe and future glory strangely mixed in Isaiah 10. But in Isaiah 11 we see the picture of the glory of the future kingdom which Christ is coming to establish on this earth. Some day He is coming to Jerusalem to sit upon the throne of David and peace shall cover the earth *as the waters cover the sea.*

Read every word of Isaiah 11 and 12, which gives a picture of this coming King and kingdom: the King Himself (11:1), His anointing (11:2), His righteous reign (11:3-5), His glorious kingdom (11:6-9), His gathering together of His people from the four corners of the earth (11:10-16), His kingdom worship (chap. 12).

Isaiah 13 records Babylon's doom. She was to carry Judah away captive but the prophet saw her destruction. God would keep His promise to Abraham

132

recorded in Genesis 12:3. God always brings a curse on any nation that afflicts Israel. You can follow this truth through history. God often allows nations to punish Israel for her national sins but retribution is inevitable (Deut. 30:5-7; Isa. 14:1,2; Joel 3:1-8).

Read Isaiah's prophecy about Babylon in Isaiah 13:19-22. Today there is not even the tent of an Arab pitched there. Only bats and owls make their home in its ruins. Not a shepherd is seen on the plains. There is only desolation. Yes, God's Word is true!

In Isaiah 14:28 we read that King Ahaz died. But Isaiah warned the people that this death must not be hailed as the end of their burdens. Even worse oppressors than Ahaz were yet to come (14:28-32).

UNDER HEZEKIAH Isaiah 15—66

The reign of Hezekiah occupied one of the most important periods in all of Israel's history. Hezekiah was a godly king. The Assyrian armies, like a dark storm cloud, were threatening the northern frontiers. Before Hezekiah had completed his sixth year, Samaria had fallen beneath this invader. This success only whetted the Assyrian appetite for further conquest. Eight years later Judah was invaded. Assyrian history tells us the first invasion was by Sargon and the second by his son, Sennacherib.

The watchmen on the walls of Jerusalem could see these stony-hearted Assyrian warriors advance by the smoke of the burning towns and cities. Hezekiah stripped the Temple of its treasures and took the gold from its doors and pillars in order to send them 300 talents of silver and 30 talents of gold to buy them off (2 Kings 18:13-16). In desperation, help from Egypt was sought. But nothing availed in face of the fury of these Assyrians.

Finally the Assyrians built their camp fires around the city of Jerusalem and demanded its surrender. Read the dramatic account of the parleyings between the Assyrian general and the chiefs of Jerusalem. See the account of the swift and terrible disaster that fell upon the Assyrians as they were mysteriously slain (Isa. 37:36-38).

Isaiah denounced the alliance with Egypt and said it was relying on horses and trusting in chariots instead of the Lord (31:1). Is it not true that we today have put our trust in the "horses and chariots" of war's machinery? Have we not multiplied our horses and chariots beyond the wildest dreams of Egypt and Babylon? We have hitched all the forces of nature to our chariots. We have armored tanks and jet airplanes, battleships and atomic carriers and submarines. We have added nuclear missiles!

History reveals a graveyard of the nations that have gone down to death through their own moral rottenness. Egypt, Babylon, and Rome are memorable examples of this. God wants us to recognize Him in national affairs. He calls His people to turn to Him (see Isa. 31:6). As a people we must get right with God before we can get right with other nations.

Isaiah spent his life trying to get Judah to become acquainted with God and His Word. He wanted them to trust wholly in God's guidance. Isn't this a worthy aim for any Christian today?

GLORIOUS FUTURE—RESTORATION!

Chapters 46—66 of Isaiah are called the "Book of

Consolation" because Isaiah tells not only of the restoration of Judah but the coming of Jehovah's "Servant" to be the Messiah King. Isaiah 53 gives us a perfect picture of our suffering Redeemer.

Can you repeat verse 5 and say, *He was pierced through for [my] transgressions, he was crushed for [my] iniquities; the chastening for [my] well-being fell upon Him, and by His scourging [I] am healed?* It is accepting this great fact that makes you a child of God. He was wounded, bruised, pierced—not for His own sins, but for ours. He bore on His own body the sins of the world.

Isaiah 60-66 tells of the coming kingdom—the future glory of Israel. God's goodness to redeemed Israel is seen in chapters 61 and 62. He promises an era of prosperity in chapters 63—65.

Minimum Daily Requirements/Spiritual Vitamins
Sunday: God's case against Judah (Isa. 1:1-18)
Monday: Isaiah's commission (Isa. 6:1-13)
Tuesday: Israel's hope (Isa. 7:10-16; 9:1-21)
Wednesday: The coming kingdom (Isa. 11:1-16)
Thursday: A great God (Isa. 40:1-31)
Friday: Christ our substitute (Isa. 53:1-12)
Saturday: A glorious salvation (Isa. 55:1-13)

Jeremiah and His Lamentations

Jeremiah prophesied to the Southern Kingdom of Judah before the exile and during the captivity. He saw five kings upon the throne of Judah: Josiah, Jehoahaz, Jehoiakim, Jehoiachin and Zedekiah. He was to Josiah what Isaiah had been to Hezekiah. Read 2 Kings 21:1-25 for the history of Jeremiah's time.

Jeremiah came from the village of Anathoth, near Jerusalem. His father, Hilkiah, was a priest. (Some think that this was "Hilkiah the priest" of 2 Kings 22.) God appointed this young man to be His prophet in this most trying hour.

Jeremiah, unlike many of the prophets, has much to say concerning himself. (Read Jer. 1:1-8.) He tells us that he was a priest by birth (1:1). He was called by the Lord to be a prophet at an early age (1:6). He pleaded his youth (he was only 21); inexperience, and lack of eloquence (1:6) as reasons for not accepting the call. Jeremiah was assured that Jehovah ordained him to this work before his birth (1:5). God has a plan for each one of our lives (see Eph. 2:10).

ANALYSIS OF JEREMIAH

Jeremiah's commission was worldwide, including not only his own country, but also Egypt, Ammon, Moab, Tyre and Sidon. He was to root out, pull down, destroy and throw down. He must root out the idolatry and pride, but he must finally "build and plant." Furthermore Jeremiah was to go only to those persons to whom the Lord sent him, and he was to say only what the Lord commanded him to say. This must be true of us also if we are to be true workers together with God.

Because the Book of Jeremiah is not arranged chronologically a division of the book is difficult. Jeremiah used many symbols given him by Jehovah in teaching the people. On one occasion he wore a rotted girdle; another time he put a yoke on his neck like an ox; again, he broke a bottle in the presence of the ruler; he bought a field and buried the deed. The interpretation is given in the text.

Here is a list of object lessons found in the book: the almond rod (chap. 1), the boiling pot (chap. 1); the rotted girdle (chap. 13), the full bottle (chap. 13), the drought (chap. 14), the potter's vessel (chap. 18), the broken bottle (chap. 19), two baskets of figs (chap. 24), bonds and yokes (chap. 27), buying a field (chap. 32), hidden stones (chap. 43), a book sunk in the Euphrates (chap. 51).

Christ is pictured in Jeremiah as the fountain of

Living Waters (2:13), Great Physician (8:22), Good Shepherd (31:10; 23:4); Righteous Branch (23:5), Redeemer (50:34), Lord our Righteousness (23:6).

BEFORE THE FALL OF JERUSALEM
Jeremiah 2—39

The prophecies of Jeremiah before the fall of Jerusalem were made in this order: prophecies in the reign of Josiah (2—12); of Jehoiakim (13—20; 25:1—27:11); of Zedekiah (21—24; 27:12—39:18). Long silences divide these.

Reign of Josiah Jeremiah 2—12

Jeremiah 2—6 tell of Judah's sin and give God's call to repentance. Jeremiah 7—9 include threatenings and the prophet's grief. Jeremiah 10—12 tell of the Lord's disappointment in His people when idolatry and disobedience continue.

In the early years of his ministry, during the reign of Josiah, Jeremiah's message, for the most part, was a warning to Judah and a call to her to repent. (Read Jer. 3:6,12,13,22,23.) He spared nothing in exposing the moral rottenness of the people (7:1-26). He warned them of coming judgments if they would not return to God. He especially told them of the danger from the north (4:6). He said that the avengers would come like a raging lion from the thicket (4:7). They would sweep over the land with chariots like the whirlwind and with horses swifter than eagles, spread terror before them and leave ruin behind (4:13).

We do not know much of Jeremiah's work during the later years of Josiah's reign. No doubt he was in great sympathy with this young reformer, but he realized that his work did not go deep enough. In the death of the good King Josiah at the battle of Megiddo, Judah suffered a calamity from which she never recovered. It was in this battle that Judah made a noble attempt to withstand the Egyptian army advancing against Assyria under Pharaoh Necho.

King Josiah was succeeded by his younger brother Jehoahaz whom "the people of the land" placed on the throne instead of the older brother Eliakim. But Jehoahaz was to reign only three months. He was deposed by Necho and carried off in chains to Egypt, where he died. Necho now appointed Jehoiakim to be ruler.

Reign of Jehoiakim Jeremiah 13—20; 25:1—27:11

In substance Jeremiah predicted the judgment of the nations and Judah. He reproved the false prophets. He foretold the Babylonian captivity.

It was a sad day for Judah when Jehoiakim ascended to power. It was a bad day for Jeremiah, too. Read what God said to Jeremiah at the beginning of Jehoiakim's reign (26:1-7). Jehoiakim was a bad ruler. He weighed the land down with taxes to meet the demands of his Egyptian conqueror (2 Kings 23:35). He was indifferent to the suffering of his people. He devoted most of his time to enlarging and adorning his palace.

During the fourth year of Jehoiakim, Jeremiah first put his prophecies in writing (36:1,2). His friend Baruch, who was such a comfort to him through his trials, took down the prophet's words. Then, since Jeremiah was imprisoned, he sent Baruch to read *the words of the Lord* in the Temple (36:3,8).

The Royal Investigating Committee immediately sent for Baruch and commanded him to read the scroll again (36:14,15). They decided the scroll must be brought to the king (36:16). However, knowing the character of this ruler, they advised Jeremiah and Baruch to go into hiding before the scroll was read in the royal presence (36:19).

The scene changes. We are no longer in the dark dungeon, but in the winter palace of Jehoiakim, surrounded by all the luxury of an Eastern court. The king is sitting before his hearth. A fire is burning. Jehudi is reading the scroll of Jeremiah. All are listening intently. When three or four pages have been read Jehoiakim can stand no more. With penknife and angry hands he cuts the scroll to pieces and throws it into the fire.

The very act of Jehoiakim seemed to symbolize the doom of the city, the Temple and all the people of Judah. They had heard God's Word and had rejected it. (See Jer. 36:20-26.)

Jeremiah and Baruch were ordered to be seized but God "hid them" (36:26). How often God does this for His children. He hides us under His wings and in the hollow of His hand far from harm.

Now the Lord commanded Jeremiah to take another scroll, and to write the words again (36:27,32).

Jehoiakim reigned 11 years; after his death his 18-year-old son came to the throne. But Jehoiachin's reign was short (about three months and ten days) because Nebuchadnezzar's army soon appeared at the gates of Jerusalem. After a three-month siege the city was captured. He took with him many of the princes and the leading people to Babylon. Among them were Jehoiachin and Daniel and his companions.

It was then that Jeremiah first mentioned the 70 years' captivity (Jer. 25:1-14). God told them just how long they must remain in exile.

Reign of Zedekiah Jeremiah 21—24; 27:12—39:18

Nebuchadnezzar placed Zedekiah, Jehoiakim's brother, on the throne in place of Jehoiachin. Only the poor were left in Jerusalem now. Jeremiah likens them to bad, worthless figs, in contrast to those who had gone who were good figs (Jer. 24). The picked men of the nation had been carried away and the men who were left were so weak and degenerate that the prophet Jeremiah could see nothing but doom for Jerusalem.

Zedekiah was friendly to Jeremiah, but he had no courage to make decisions of his own. He was like clay in the hands of his princes. The men who were left had taken the places of the real nobility of the nation, but they were not qualified to govern.

Jeremiah incurred the displeasure of the prophets who had gone to Babylon because in a letter to the exiles he directly opposed their prediction of an early return from captivity (29:1-4.) The prophets in Jerusalem disliked it too because they thought that soon they could throw off Nebuchadnezzar's yoke. Zedekiah's advisers were in favor of looking to Egypt for help, but Jeremiah kept insisting that the Chaldeans (Babylonians) would capture the city. (See 37:3-10.) Finally Zedekiah broke his covenant with the king of Babylon. Nebuchadnezzar swiftly marched against Jerusalem and the final siege began.

As the siege proceeded, Jeremiah's enemies charged him with desertion and thrust him into prison. They petitioned the king to put him to death (38:4). Weakling that he was, Zedekiah gave Jeremiah over into the hands of the princes. For some reason they shrank from killing him. But they chose a worse thing for Jeremiah. They lowered him into a miry dungeon, and left him to die of starvation and exposure. But God was with him. An Ethiopian, Ebed-melech, heard of Jeremiah's plight and made his way to the king. Gaining permission, he rushed to the dungeon and lowered old rags for the prophet to put under his armpits beneath the cords, for Jeremiah had sunk in the mire and the work of getting him out would mean a great strain (38:6-13).

After Jeremiah's deliverance Zedekiah, driven by fear, visited Jeremiah to find out what was in store for him. Jeremiah could only promise him doom for the city. Jeremiah still insisted that the king should surrender to Nebuchadnezzar, but Zedekiah was afraid of the princes (38:14-28).

AFTER THE FALL OF JERUSALEM Jeremiah 40—52

After 18 months of siege, Jerusalem was taken, Zedekiah's sons were put to death before his eyes, and he was blinded and carried in chains to Babylon (39:1-7). Jeremiah was given the choice of going to Babylon where freedom and honor awaited him, but he stayed with the remnant left in the land (39:11,12; 40:1-16).

Finally those left in Jerusalem fled to Egypt in spite of God's warning against it (Jer. 43). They asked Jeremiah to pray for guidance, but when it was given they refused to obey it. The prophet and Baruch were compelled to accompany them. Even in Egypt we find the prophet carrying out his commission. He prophesied the conquest of Egypt by Nebuchadnezzar (43:8-13) and warned against idolatry (44:26-28). This is the last we hear of Jeremiah. How long he lived in Egypt afterwards we do not know.

JEREMIAH AND HIS TIMES

Jeremiah's life was one of gloom. He had to watch the people and city which he loved fall from sin to sin. And all the time he had no hope that things might change. How deeply he felt all this can be seen in his Lamentations. Other prophets had at least occasional successes to cheer them in the midst of difficulties, but Jeremiah seemed to be fighting a losing battle to the very end. He preached to deaf ears and seemed to reap only hate in return for his love for his people. In life he seemed to accomplish little. But God has given us a record that makes him one of the greatest of all the prophets.

JEREMIAH'S LAMENTATIONS

Here is another of the Bible's exquisite books of poetry. It is commonly attributed to Jeremiah. Five beautiful, distinct poems are bound together in the book. It is not all sorrow. Above the clouds of the poet's weeping over the sins of his people, God's sun is shining. In Lamentations 8:22-27 the light breaks through. God's grace always shines above the clouds of sin (see Rom. 5:20), and it will always shine in the heart which is trusting in God through faith in the Lord Jesus Christ.

Minimum Daily Requirements/Spiritual Vitamins

Sunday: Jeremiah warns Judah (Jer. 1:1-10; 2:1-13; 3:12,22,23; 4:14-19; 6:1-30)

Monday: A rebuke (Jer. 7:1-15; 9:1-16; 17:5-18)

Tuesday: The potter (Jer. 18:1-17)

Wednesday: The faithless shepherds (Jer. 23:1-40)

Thursday: Repentance and restoration (Jer. 24; 25)

Friday: Israel's last days (Jer. 30:18—31:40)

Saturday: The overthrow of Judah (Jer. 52:1-34); Comfort to the sorrowing (Lam. 1—5)

The Visions of Ezekiel

Jeremiah was the last of the prophets in Jerusalem before the exile. His ministry was still going on when the end came. Recall the story. The young prophet Ezekiel was already at work among the exiles in Babylon. God had sent a witness to the people in their captivity to warn them and to remind them why these calamities had befallen them.

You will find little of Ezekiel in the Gospels or Epistles. But look in Revelation. Ezekiel and John seem to lock arms across the centuries, and looking into the future they see the unfolding of a new heaven and a new earth.

Like Jeremiah, Ezekiel was both a prophet and a priest. When he was 25 years old he was carried captive to Babylon in 597 B.C. with the upper class of people, 11 years before the destruction of Jerusalem. For five years the captives living in the concentration camp in Babylon had no preacher. Then Ezekiel began to serve them. He immediately tried to remove their false hopes of an early return to Palestine and prepare them for the news of the tragic destruction of their beloved Jerusalem. Jeremiah remained among the Jews in Jerusalem, Ezekiel lived with the exiles in Babylon, and Daniel lived in the court of the rulers in Babylon.

BEFORE THE SIEGE Ezekiel 1—24

The "glory of God" seems to be the key phrase to Ezekiel. It occurs 12 times in the first 11 chapters. Then it does not occur again until chapter 43.

As the book opens we see Ezekiel, a young man of about 30, being commissioned by God for a great service. The prophet saw a fiery cloud approaching. In the glow were four living creatures, suggested by the cherubim of the Temple (see 1 Kings 6:23-28; Gen. 3:24; Ps. 18:10). Each had four wings and four faces: that of a man, a lion, an ox and an eagle, symbolizing intelligence, dignity, strength and speed. They faced east, west, north and south suggesting that all parts of the universe are open to the gaze of God. The wings showed that there was no spot inaccessible to divine power. There were eyes in the wheels—wheels so equipped cannot miss their way. We see a symbol of the omnipotence (all power), omnipresence (all presence), and omniscience (all knowledge) of God.

The mysterious whir of the mighty wings was followed by an equally mysterious silence. The wings dropped. The chariots stopped. Above the heads of the creatures was a crystal floor on which rested a sapphire throne, and on the throne Almighty God Himself, a figure of supernatural brilliance and glory. The terror of divine majesty was softened by a lovely rainbow around the throne. Little wonder that when Ezekiel saw this vision he fell prostrate.

Following the vision the silence was broken by God telling the prostrate prophet to rise and accept his commission for service. God wants more than inactive submission. He wants loving service. Ezekiel was called to declare the message of God—a message of doom to the people (read Ezek. 2:1-10).

The prophet's authority is suggested by the symbolic swallowing of a scroll. He must make the message his own. He must "eat it" (3:3). Bitter as its contents were to his mouth, they were sweet as honey, for it is sweet to do the will of God and to be trusted with tasks for Him.

Then the whir of the wings and the roar of the wheels was heard and the chariot departed. The prophet found his way to Tel-abib, a colony of his fellow exiles and remained for a week.

The Watchman

At the end of the week he received another message from God. This time he was called to be a watchman (3:16-21). As a watchman Ezekiel was to warn individual men of the coming catastrophe. Each person must repent. Each one must hear the Word. How true this is today of every person. Each person must accept Christ for himself. No one can do it for another (see John 3:16; 5:24).

Four Symbols of Coming Doom

1. The siege of Jerusalem (Ezek. 4:2,3): Ezekiel cannot speak, but he is still a prophet and can preach, if not by word, by symbol. (See 3:22-27.)

2. The exile duration (4:4-8): Ezekiel lay upon his side to symbolize the years of punishment the Jews were to suffer in exile—a day for each year.

3. The hardships of the exiles (4:9-17): The famine due to siege is symbolized here by the prophet's food and drink, carefully measured out.

4. The fate of the besieged (5:1-17): This last symbol, the knife and razor, is the most terrible. It suggests the completeness of the destruction.

DURING THE SIEGE OF JERUSALEM Ezekiel 25—32

Ezekiel's gloomy predictions are fulfilled. But with the news of the fall of Jerusalem he immediately begins to prophesy about the future restoration of Israel. God often reveals a bright picture of Israel's future against the backdrop of divine judgment (see Ezek. 33—48). But before Israel is restored to her land those who are her enemies must be put out of the way. So at this point Ezekiel writes of the future doom of these foreign powers.

First he speaks of her neighbors who have insulted and harassed her. God pronounces His judgment upon Ammon and Moab for their sins against Israel. From Israel's petty neighbors with their petty spite, Ezekiel turns to the great empires of Tyre, Sidon and Egypt. Ezekiel describes the brilliance of Tyre, the extent of her commerce, the pity and terror inspired by her fall. Ezekiel 29—32 tells of the collapse of Egypt. Nebuchadnezzar with his terrible army will deal the crushing blow.

AFTER THE SIEGE Ezekiel 33—48

Ezekiel now looks into the future and sees the final

restoration and glory of Israel when God will gather together His scattered people. Shepherds of Israel had proven faithless to the people, the flock had been scattered; but Jehovah would set up a Shepherd, "my servant David" (34:23,24). This, no doubt, refers to the Messiah. Look up 2 Samuel 7:16; Psalm 89:20-36; Isaiah 7:13,14; 9:6,7; 11:1-12; Jeremiah 23:2-7; Ezekiel 37:21-28; Hosea 3:4,5; Luke 1:30-33; Acts 2:29-31; 15:14-17. All reveal that the future blessing of Israel will come with the Messiah, David's Son. When the Jews rejected Jesus, they did not thwart God's plan or defeat His purpose for in Acts we read that Christ was raised from the dead to sit on David's throne, and He will return for that purpose (Acts 2:30).

The restoration that Ezekiel tells about does not refer to the feeble remnant that returned to Jerusalem after the 70 years of captivity (see Ezra and Neh.), for it is a restoration from all nations (Ezek. 36:24).

Ezekiel sees a vision of a valley of dry bones (37:1-14). The "bones" are the Jews who shall be alive at the restoration of the nation. The graves are the nations where they are dwelling. God first will bring them into their own land. Then they will be converted—a nation shall be born in a day. The resurrection in this chapter is not of the individual Jew but of the whole nation.

Ezekiel 38 opens with the doom of *Gog, of the land of Magog*. The reference is to the northern (European) powers, perhaps headed up by Russia. Read these passages in connection with Zechariah 14:1-9; 12:1-4; Matthew 24:14-30; Revelation 14:14-20; 19:17-21. Ezekiel also gives the description of the kingdom during the coming millennial age. This is what the 1000-year reign of Christ on earth is called when He shall sit upon the throne of David in Jerusalem (see Rev. 20:6). All the prophets tell us of what a glorious day this will be for both Jew and Gentile. We read of the Temple, the worship, and the final possession of the land given to Abraham and to his seed according to the covenant God gave to him (see Gen. 12:1-3; 13:14,15; 15:18; 17:3-8).

In the Old Testament, while the Jews were in what seemed hopeless captivity, God declared constantly that He would restore the Jews to their own land and set up the throne and the kingdom of David through David's greater Son. With His reign will come such earthly and spiritual blessings as have not been known since the world began.

Minimum Daily Requirements/Spiritual Vitamins
Sunday: The prophet's call (Ezek. 2:1—3:9)
Monday: The prophet a watchman (Ezek. 3:10-27)
Tuesday: Israel saved (Ezek. 11:14-21; 28:25,26)
Wednesday: Israel's sins (Ezek. 22:3-31)
Thursday: Israel's future (Ezek. 34:1-31)
Friday: Israel's restoration (Ezek. 36:1-38)
Saturday: Vision of the dry bones (Ezek. 37:1-14)

Daniel, God's Statesman and Prophet

Daniel has been called the prophet of dreams to whom God revealed His secrets (Dan. 2:19). Daniel, like Ezekiel, looks far into the future. One cannot understand the great signs of Revelation without looking at their meaning in Daniel.

Daniel belonged to a family of high rank. He was carried to Babylon during the first deportation of the captives. There he gained a high position and was influential throughout the 70 years of his captivity. He saw his captive brothers return to Jerusalem under the decree of Cyrus. He saw world-ruling Babylon pass away and a new empire arise. Even at the age of 90 he received a position of high distinction in the court of Persia.

Daniel's whole life from the time of his captivity was spent in the city of Babylon. There he lived a life without blame and was well favored. Although Daniel was a captive, he rose to be prime minister of Babylon. The wonderful thing is that he always remained true to Jehovah God. Ezekiel refers to him as a model of righteousness (Ezek. 14:14-20; 28:3).

REIGN OF NEBUCHADNEZZAR Daniel 1—4

Daniel, Hananiah, Mishael, and Azariah (also called Shadrach, Meshach, Abed-nego) had been taken captive from Jerusalem by Nebuchadnezzar to his palace in Babylon. Daniel was only about 16 years old, Nebuchadnezzar was a little older. He came to the throne about the time that Daniel was taken captive into Babylon, and was the most powerful and distinguished king of the Babylonian empire.

Daniel and his friends lived in an atmosphere of loose morals and low standards even though they were in a palace. Evils much like those of today were rampant everywhere. Yet we read that they kept themselves apart from the evil of that court—true to God in a day when everything was against them.

The youths were brought very quickly face to face with a serious practical difficulty. As "favored ones," they lived in the palace and were given many of the delicacies of the king's table. They were to be trained in state affairs and equipped for high positions. It was hard indeed to refuse the king's meat and ask for a simpler fare. However, the king's meat had probably been offered in sacrifice to idols (Exod. 34:15; 1 Cor. 10:20), and the flesh food would have been killed with the blood left in the animal (Lev. 3:17; 7:26). Both kinds of meats were forbidden by God. They asked to be allowed to prove that their faces would not look starved if they didn't eat the meat. And God gave them favor in the eyes of their companions. Remember, we ought always to obey God rather than men.

The Dream of World Empires Daniel 2

God's power is shown through His dealing with Daniel and his three companions in the wisdom and understanding He gave them. There was a stir in the palace when Nebuchadnezzar had a dream and not one of the wise men could tell him what it was. A decree was made that all the wise men should be slain including Daniel and his friends.

Daniel called his prayer partners (Dan. 2:17) and they presented their problem to God and God showed Daniel the dream and its interpretation.

Nebuchadnezzar's dream and the interpretation teach us some interesting things about the history of the world from that time till the "end of this age." God had revealed the future to a heathen monarch.

Picture a great image. The head was of gold, its breast and arms of silver, the belly and thighs of brass, and its legs of iron, with its feet and toes of iron and clay. Then a stone cut out without hands hit the image and broke it to pieces; and the stone became a great mountain and filled the whole earth. Daniel 2:38 says that the head of gold is Babylon. The Medo-Persians (silver) were to follow (8:20) and Greece (brass) was to follow Persia (8:21). Daniel 9:26 indicates a fourth world-power (iron). From then on we find an ever-dividing kingdom and a government which will divide into many kingdoms (the toes). Deterioration is represented by the feet and toes being part iron and part clay which cannot hold together. This last government will be the weakest. It will not be completely unified, and will finally end in chaos.

In the "Stone" cut out without hands we see

Christ, whose kingdom shall never be destroyed, bringing to an end all the other kingdoms. Christ will come and set up a kingdom which will last forever (2:44,45). For an interesting study, see what the Word says about the "Stone" in Psalm 118:22; Isaiah 8:14; 28:16; Zechariah 3:9.

The great King Nebuchadnezzar fell on his face and worshiped Daniel, and declared that his God was the God of all gods. But this wonderful revelation of God had little real effect upon Nebuchadnezzar. It did not bring him to his knees before God.

The Fiery Furnace Daniel 3

Yes, here they are again, after 20 years. Nebuchadnezzar had set up a golden image on the plain of Dura and commanded all people to fall down and worship it. If any refused, he should be cast into a fiery furnace. But there were three in the throng who refused to obey the king—Shadrach, Meshach and Abed-nego. Spies reported their disobedience.

The story of the fiery furnace is a familiar one. What was the wonderful thing about that scene? The Son of God was with them. What effect did this have on Nebuchadnezzar? He was filled with great admiration for the miraculous power of the God of these men. But still he did not bow to worship God in humility. He calls Jehovah "their God." Remember God wants us to say, "My Lord, and my God."

The King Dreams Again Daniel 4

God gave Nebuchadnezzar the image representing the Gentile kingdoms and showed him his doom, but he did not repent. Then God spoke to him from the fiery furnace where He revealed His power, but still his proud heart felt no repentance.

Now God speaks to Nebuchadnezzar for the third time in the dream of the great tree which was cut down (4:4-27). This was a warning to Nebuchadnezzar of his coming madness. God was trying to bring this proud king to worship Him. But a year later we see him a madman, his mind gone. He fancied himself a beast (4:28-34). All this because he had set himself up as a rival against Almighty God (see Dan. 4:30).

Through his insanity, Nebuchadnezzar's eyes were opened and his conscience was touched. He confessed to the greatness and goodness of God (4:34). He learned that man is not the architect of his own fortune.

REIGN OF BELSHAZZAR Daniel 5,7,8

As chapter 5 opens we see a great banquet hall with 1000 lords sitting about the tables. As an extra feature, Belshazzar (grandson of Nebuchadnezzar) had sent for the sacred golden and silver vessels which his grandfather Nebuchadnezzar had stripped from the Temple in Jerusalem. To show just how little he regarded the God of Israel, the last prince of Babylon, Belshazzar, drank wine to the idols in these sacred vessels.

God showed His power in the awful handwriting on the wall. Daniel was called in to explain the meaning. The prophet fearlessly condemned this foolish and sensual young king. Read the details of the divine interruption in Daniel 5.

Many of the tablets from Babylon, recently found, tell us that the Persian army took Babylon without a battle. Four months later Cyrus entered the city. Darius probably received the kingdom from Cyrus and was vice-regent over some part of it.

Daniel's Vision

During the first year of Belshazzar's reign, Daniel had a vision of four wild beasts, which symbolized the four kingdoms pictured in Nebuchadnezzar's dream (chap. 7).

In Nebuchadnezzar's dream-image we have man's view of the magnificence of these kingdoms. In Daniel's dream we have God's view of the same. See who Daniel says these four beasts are in Daniel 7:17-23. The first, or Babylon, was like a lion with eagle's wings. (Jeremiah likened Nebuchadnezzar both to the lion and eagle in Jer. 49:19-22.) Persia was the bear, the cruel animal who delights to kill for the sake of killing. The third was a leopard or panther, a beast of prey. His four wings portray swiftness. Here we see the rapid marches of Alexander's army and his insatiable love of conquest. In 13 short years he had conquered the world. The fourth beast was different from all the rest. He was *dreadful and terrifying and extremely strong; and it had large iron teeth* according to Daniel 7:7.

Two years later in Daniel 8 we have another vision, this time of a ram and a he-goat. This vision includes only two of the four kingdoms, Persia and Greece (see Dan. 8:20,21).

REIGN OF DARIUS Daniel 6,9

Twenty-three years after the death of Nebuchadnezzar, his great city, Babylon, fell into the hands of the Medes. Even under these new rulers, Daniel was in a place of power. The jealousy of the other officials was aroused by the preference given to Daniel, and a plot to destroy him was quickly formed.

The officials knew that the king would not lift a finger against Daniel, so they had to trap the king. What was their bait? Read Daniel 6:7—9. Notice the subtle appeal to the king's pride.

The law of the Medes and Persians was unchangeable (see Esther 1:19; 8:8). The king saw that he had been deceived, and realizing the injustice of putting Daniel to death, did his best to avoid carrying out the law. Notice that when Daniel found out that the writing was signed, he did not fall down in terror and agony, but he praised and thanked God. (Read Dan. 6:10; Phil. 4:6,7.)

REIGN OF CYRUS Daniel 10—12

It was during the reign of Cyrus that the decree was sent out for the captives to return and build the walls of Jerusalem. (Read Ezra 1:2-4.) Daniel, now nearly 90 years old, was too aged to return. He had outlived the friends and companions of his youth. Now he saw the Israelites gathering in the streets of Babylon and the aged man watched the last caravan leave for Jerusalem. Daniel was concerned about his people. We see how he was comforted in his perplexity in Daniel 10.

The Last Days

In Daniel 11 the vision concerns the near future of the kingdom in which Daniel was so great a personage. Three kings were yet to come in the Medo-

Persian empire. Then Alexander, the mighty king of Greece, would appear (see Dan. 11:2,3). His empire would be divided among his four generals. The course of affairs is followed down to Antiochus Epiphanes (the "little horn" of Dan. 8). His desecration of the sanctuary is again mentioned in Daniel 12:11.

The great tribulation follows (12:1). This is a time of unparalleled trouble. What does our Lord say of it in Matthew 24:21? Mention is made of two resurrections (read Dan. 12:2). These two will be 1000 years apart (Rev. 20:1-6). The first is the resurrection of the saints at Christ's coming to life everlasting. This is followed by 1000 years, called the millennium. Then the resurrection of the wicked to shame everlasting.

Minimum Daily Requirements/Spiritual Vitamins
Sunday: Daniel the captive (Dan. 1,2)
Monday: Nebuchadnezzar, the king (Dan. 3,4)
Tuesday: Belshazzar's reign (Dan. 5; 7; 8)
Wednesday: Darius' reign (Dan. 6,9)
Thursday: God's glory (Dan. 10)
Friday: The conflict of kings (Dan. 11)
Saturday: Daniel's last message (Dan. 12)

The Early Prophets (Hosea, Joel, Amos)

With the study of Hosea's prophecy we enter 12 books known as the minor prophets. The difference between the major and minor prophets is not a matter of importance but of the amount written.

Hosea was sent to the 10 northern tribes called "Israel." He lived and prophesied in the Northern Kingdom of Israel when the splendors of Jeroboam II's brilliant reign of 41 years was beginning to fade into the black midnight of Israel's captivity. He prophesied during the eighth century B.C. (Rome and Carthage were both founded during this period.)

Hosea's contemporaries were Amos, Isaiah and Micah. He has been called the Jeremiah of the Northern Kingdom. In Hosea "Israel" means the 10 tribes that formed the Northern Kingdom. "Judah" means the tribes of Judah and Benjamin that formed the Southern Kingdom.

Israel's Unfaithfulness Hosea 1—3

The hero of this book, Hosea, is one of the greatest

lovers in all literature. We find his love so strong that even the worst actions of an unfaithful wife could not kill it. Read Hosea 1:1 for a bit of the personal history of the prophet.

We know little about Hosea other than that he had a sad home life. The book pictures this man as gentle, frank and affectionate. He had a deep loving nature that made him attached to his home. Hosea was not trained in a seminary (school of the prophets), but he was a layman called by God to give the message to Israel that God loved them.

As chapter 1 opens, Hosea is told to marry a harlot (Hos. 1:2,3). God was using this for a sign to His people of how they remained the object of Jehovah's love, in spite of their sinfulness. It was a picture of His redeeming grace. Grace is unmerited favor. Israel was undeserving of Jehovah's love, yet He still lavished love upon them.

Hosea obeyed God (1:3). He gave all he had to Gomer. In return, Hosea's name, domestic reputation and love were all sacrificed on the altar of a shameful woman. How like our Lord Jesus this is! He not only came to us while we were yet in sin but He died the death of shame on Calvary for us that all He had might be ours (see Titus 2:14).

Gomer ran away from home and left her young husband Hosea with two little boys and a daughter to care for. Still loving her, he tried everything to win her back to a happy family life. But she would not. What a sad picture of man's stubbornness! What a wonderful picture of God's love!

Just as Hosea was married to unfaithful Gomer, so God was married to unfaithful Israel. Hosea's experience helped him understand God's heart of love as He yearned for wayward Israel to return to Him.

Israel's Sin and Chastisement Hosea 4—10

Two hundred years earlier, the 20 tribes had seceded from Judah and set up an independent kingdom called Israel. They immediately began worshiping idols. God sent Elijah and then Elisha to warn them, but they refused to return to God. Now we hear a new voice, Hosea! Read his message in Hosea 6:1.

Hosea, whose name means "salvation," was poet laureate to the king. But he was more than that. He was God's voice to the people. But the backslidden nation did not care to hear that God was grieved by His children's sins. Remember the name of Israel connected with sin or backsliding which is used 37 times in this book—it is Ephraim.

Israel's Hope Hosea 11—14

Light breaks over these last chapters. They show us Israel's ultimate blessings in the future kingdom and we get a glimpse into God's heart of love. God did not choose Israel for His people because they were the greatest or richest of the nations of the world (Deut. 7:6-8). He rather chose a weak, unattractive slave child to be the object of His love, care and blessings (Hos. 11:1). But Israel began to grow persistently disobedient and rebellious. The more the prophets warned them the further they went away from God. They showed no gratitude to God for all their blessings. In their freedom they forgot God and fell into sin and idolatry and were plunging into captivity (11:2).

Hosea 14 is the greatest chapter in the Bible for backsliders. Read the wonderful words of the Lord to backsliding Israel in Hosea 14:4. God's great heart is bursting with love, but our sins keep us from experiencing all that is there. As with Israel, you may know the joy of barriers broken down and love poured out (14:5). See how God pictures His abiding joy in His people after they are healed (14:5-8).

JOEL AND THE PLAGUE

Joel is considered to be one of the earliest prophets whose writings have come down to us. He possibly knew both Elijah and Elisha in his youth. His personal history is stated in Joel 1:1. His name means "Jehovah is my God." He ministered to Judah just a little before Hosea prophesied to Israel.

Joel has been called "the prophet of religious revival." He knew that revival must follow repentance and he tried to bring Judah to this place.

Appalling famine, caused by a plague of locusts, followed by a prolonged drought devastated the land. People and flocks were dying for lack of food and water. Joel graphically described the plague, calling the old men to confirm the fact that there had never been one like it before (1:2). Drunkards felt the effect because the vines had been destroyed (1:5). Priests had no meat-offering nor drink-offering of wine to offer (1:9). Cattle and sheep suffered (1:20).

Then Joel called the people to consider the cause of the calamity. They must mourn with true penitence and fasting if they wished to be spared further judgment. Desperate, they were ready to listen to anyone who could explain their plight. It was a great hour for in their extremity men would turn to God.

The Fast—The Promise

The blast of the ram's horn calling an assembly for a great fast opens this chapter (2:1). Everyone is there —old and young alike. Even brides and bridegrooms on their wedding day attend (2:16). The priests come in black sackcloth, and bow to the ground and cry to God within the sanctuary. It was an event to bring the people back to God (2:12).

The locusts had made an Eden into a desolate wilderness (2:3). For one who has not seen it, an army of locusts is incredible. They fill the air and darken the sun like an eclipse (2:2). They spread for miles over the land. Armies of "soldiers" advance, destroying everything that is green. In a few minutes every leaf and blade is destroyed. Others follow stripping the bark from the trees (1:6,7). The people dig trenches, kindle fires and beat and burn to death heaps of insects, but the effort is useless. After the country is stripped, they go into cities, march into houses (2:4,7-9) and consume everything that can be consumed. A land that has been devastated by locusts takes years to recover. God's promise, *I will make up to you for the years that the swarming locust has eaten* (2:25) becomes more graphic in the mind when one sees the desolation wrought by the consuming insects.

The prophet assures the people that God will indeed send both temporal mercies (2:18-27) and spiritual blessings (2:28-32).

Spiritual deliverance is the great central promise of the Book of Joel. Other prophets have foretold details concerning the Lord's life on earth and even His future reign. To Joel was committed the privilege of telling that He would pour out His Spirit upon all flesh. He tells us that the blessing will flow forth from Jerusalem. This prophecy was fulfilled at Pentecost (Acts 2:1-21).

There is a lesson for us today. The church is in a desolate condition. It has been laid waste by many spiritual foes. There are famine and drought on all sides. The call goes to Christians today to go into the dust before the Lord in true repentance of heart. This repentance must begin with ministers and lay leaders. If we will return unto the Lord, He will fulfill His promise to us by His outpouring of the Holy Spirit and then He will restore *the years that the swarming locust has eaten.*

The day of the Lord, spoken of five times in this short book, refers to judgment. Joel tells of a series of judgments: the present locusts, the armies of invasion which were about to come as a scourge of God upon the land, and the final day of the Lord described in chapter 3. The day of the Lord is the period of time from the return of the Lord in glory until the new heavens and the new earth (Isa. 2:17-20; 13:6-9; Jer. 46:10; 1 Cor. 5:1-5).

Blessings for the Future

They include enemies overthrown (3:1-15), Jerusalem delivered (3:16,17), the land blessed (3:18) and Judah restored (3:19-21). Only God could have told Joel of the return of the Jews from captivity. Joel not only saw the return from Babylon, but the last regathering of the Jews from among the Gentile nations. He also tells of the judgment of the nations after the battle of Armageddon (3:2-7). (Read Matt. 25:32 and Rev. 19:17-21.)

After Israel has been restored and the nations of the earth have been judged (3:1,2) then the everlasting kingdom will be set up (3:20). Once again the land of promise will be the center of power. Christ will return to establish His rule as sovereign. God will dwell in Zion (3:17).

AMOS, THE SHEPHERD

Amos was from Tekoa, a small town about 12 miles south of Jerusalem. He was not a prophet nor the son of a prophet. He was not a priest nor a member of the prophets' school. He was a sheepherder and grower of sycamore trees (Amos 7:14).

On the wild uplands of Judah, behind Tekoa, Amos received his training as a prophet straight from the hand of God. His beautiful writing abounds with illustrations from his mountain home. Like David, he had gazed on the stars and looked beyond to their Creator. He was not a courtier like Isaiah, nor a priest like Jeremiah, but just an ordinary working man.

Amos was not the only prophet of his day. God sent a galaxy of messengers to save His people from the destruction they were inevitably facing. No doubt, as a boy, he had known Jonah and possibly Elisha. Hosea was his co-worker. When Amos' work was coming to a close, Isaiah and Micah appeared.

Amos prophesied while Uzziah was on the throne of Judah, and Jeroboam II was king of Israel. This was a time of great prosperity. The old boundaries of the kingdom of David were gained back, money poured in and armies were victorious. Amos and

Hosea were prophets to Israel (Northern Kingdom) and Isaiah and Micah to the Southern Kingdom (Judah).

Judgment Against Nations Amos 1,2

Amos started his preaching to the assembled crowds at Bethel by proclaiming the Lord's judgment upon six neighboring nations—Damascus (Syria), Gaza (Philistia), Tyrus (Phoenicia), Edom, Ammon and Moab. Then he came nearer home and pronounced judgment against Judah (2:4) and against Israel itself (2:6). Amos' approach was clever. We are always willing to hear of our enemy's doom. Our own is harder to swallow.

When the people doubted his authority, Amos gave a series of seven questions to show that the Lord had revealed His secret to him. Therefore he must prophesy (3:3-8).

Amos denounced the sin of Israel more graphically than Hosea. He spoke of their careless ease and luxury, their oppression of the poor, the lying and cheating that existed, and worse than all, their hypocrisy in worship.

Judgment Against Israel Amos 3—6

Amos was called to tell of certain punishment if Israel rejected the repeated warning of God. He told Israel they were greedy, unjust, unclean and profane, and that they defended and excused themselves on the ground that they were God's chosen people. The Israelites boasted that because they were the chosen nation no real evil could befall them. We see many professing Christians today in the same danger. They imagine their salvation is secured by their being members of a church. They are conferring a favor upon God and He cannot condemn them.

Amos condemned Israel, the chosen nation. They knew God's law. Therefore their sin was the greater. Amos denounced their injustice in the administration of the law. They had forgotten righteousness. The rich were cruel and longed to see the poor oppressed. Even the religious sacrifices and feasts of the people became an abomination (5:21). When they made their pilgrimages from Gilgal to Bethel, they only sinned the more because it was merely an outward form mixed with idolatry. God demands conduct worthy of Himself, not just empty sacrifices.

God always warns before a punishment. Yes, and offers a way of escape. God denounces sin, but He offers a remedy for sin. Amos called attention to how God had sent drought, plagues and earthquakes. Still they did not repent. Therefore, Israel should prepare for God's judgment (Amos 5). If Israel had sought the Lord, the *day of the Lord* spoken of in Amos 5:20 would not have overtaken them. They did not seek Him and Assyrian fighters ushered in that day.

Visions for the Future Amos 7—9

We do not know how long Amos preached in Bethel but we know that throngs heard his fearless message. When he spoke of the doom of surrounding nations, they cheered him to the last echo.

Then Amaziah, the priest of Bethel, backed by the king, told Amos to go back and mind his own business (chap. 7). Amos was silenced by the false prophet. He was driven from Israel. When Amos found that Israel would not hear him, he returned to Judah and put his writings in a book so all the people could read and understand it.

Amos, as do most of the prophets, tells us of doom but also of a bright future of God's chosen people. The whole land will once more be a kingdom under the house of David (9:11,12). The Tabernacle of David, now torn down, shall be rebuilt. Israel shall be restored to her land and prosper. A happy people shall dwell in a happy land.

Minimum Daily Requirements/Spiritual Vitamins
Sunday: Israel's willful ignorance (Hos. 4)
Monday: Israel's glorious future (Hos. 3; 14)
Tuesday: Punishment and blessing (Joel 2)
Wednesday: The restoration of Israel (Joel 3)
Thursday: Personal warnings (Amos 3:1-7; 4:6-12)
Friday: Intercession (Amos 3:1-17; 8:1-7)
Saturday: Future kingdom blessings (Amos 9:1-15)

Messages to the Nations (Obadiah, Jonah, Micah)

South of the Dead Sea and on the western border of the Arabian plateau lies a range of precipitous, red sandstone heights known as Mount Seir. It is here that Esau settled after he sold his birthright to his brother Jacob. Having driven out the Horites, he occupied the mountain (Deut. 2:12). These Horites are first spoken of in the time of Abraham (Gen. 14:5,6). Sela, or Petra (Rock) was their capital.

Petra is one of the wonders of the world. It perched like an "eagle's nest" (Obad. 1:4) amid inaccessible mountain vastness. Its only approach was through a deep rock cleft about a mile long with massive cliffs more than 700 feet high rising on either side. The city was able to withstand any invasion.

The descendants of Esau were called Edomites. They would go on raiding expeditions, and then retreat to their impregnable fortress where they kept alive in their hearts a bitter hatred of the Jews that began back with Jacob and Esau. They never failed in helping an army who attacked the Jews.

This book is the shortest in the Old Testament. It contains only 21 verses, but it includes two important themes—the doom of the proud and rebellious and the deliverance of the meek and humble.

The Doom of Edom Obadiah 1:1-16

Of the prophet who wrote this book we know nothing. His contemporary was Jeremiah. We find the occasion of this prophecy was, no doubt, the awful day when Nebuchadnezzar took Jerusalem and reduced it to a desolate heap. The Edomites had helped the marauders by catching the fleeing Israelites, treating them with cruelty and selling them as slaves (vv. 11-14).

Read what God had commanded Israel in Deuteronomy 23:7. But Edom had shown implacable hatred for Israel from the time Israel was refused passage through Edom on the way to Canaan (Num. 20:14-21) to the day of the destruction of Jerusalem by the Chaldeans when Edom cried, *Raze it, raze it* (Ps. 137:7).

Because of the pride and cruel hatred of Edom, her utter destruction was decreed (Obad. 1:3,4,10). Nothing could save the guilty nation. The people were driven from their rocky home five years after the destruction of Jerusalem when Nebuchadnezzar, passing down the valley of Arabah which formed the military road to Egypt, crushed the Edomites. They lost their existence as a nation about 150 B.C., and their name perished with the capture of Jerusalem by the Romans in A.D. 70 *As you have done, it will be done to you* (v. 15).

The book closes with the promise of deliverance for Zion. *And the house of Jacob will possess their possessions* (v. 17). The first step will be the recovery of what was previously their own. Edom will be as though she had never been—swallowed up forever. But Israel will rise again from her fall. She will possess not only her own land, but also Philistia and Edom. God's chosen people, the Jews, shall possess their possessions and among the dearest to them is their Holy Land. Obadiah, like the other prophets, also predicts the coming of the day of the Lord and the establishment of Messiah's kingdom. Remember a Christian is also an heir of promises to be fulfilled when Christ comes.

God's judgment on Edom as Israel's notable enemy should warn nations today that God has not cast off His people and that nations that oppress them will surely bring down His judgments (read Gen. 12:3).

JONAH AND NINEVEH

Jonah was a native of Gath-hepher, a town about an hour's distance from Nazareth. He lived in the reign of Jeroboam II and prophesied some of his military successes (see 2 Kings 14:25).

There are two amazing events in Jonah. One is the great fish swallowing Jonah and the other is that such a large heathen city as Nineveh was converted by an obscure foreign missionary in just a few days. See what Jesus said in Matthew 12:40,41.

Nineveh, situated on the east bank of the Tigris, 400 miles from the Mediterranean, was one of the greatest cities of the world. It was the capital of Assyria. The stronghold of the city was about 30 miles long and 10 miles wide. There were great and beautiful palaces with the finest of gardens and art. Intellectual attainments were almost incredible. But the city was as great in wickedness as it was in wealth and power.

An Obstinate Prophet Jonah 1,2

God told Jonah to arise and go to Nineveh, but Jonah fled to Tarshish *from the presence of the Lord* (Jon. 1:2,3). He said no to God. Why did he flee? Read Jonah 3:10 and 4:2. Assyria was Israel's dreaded enemy. Just when Assyria seemed to have been weakened in power, God told Jonah to go to the capital of that hostile country and pronounce judgment against it for its great wickedness. Jonah feared that Nineveh might repent and be spared impending doom. But if Assyria fell, Jonah's own beloved Israel might escape judgment at Assyria's hands.

As soon as Jonah fled, God began to act. Read events that took place before the throwing of Jonah into the sea (Jon. 1:3-15). Jonah was cast into the sea, but he was gripped by the hand of God (1:17). No doubt, two things hindered Jonah when God told him to go to Nineveh—his pride and his scorn of the rest of the world. God took this out of him in the fish's belly.

The story of Jonah 2 tells how Jonah came to the point where he confessed that he could do nothing by himself (2:9). Then God set him at liberty (2:10).

An Obedient, Perplexed Prophet Jonah 3,4

God gave Jonah another chance to be of service.

How foolish he was to make the Lord repeat His call! How much better to obey at once!

It was not easy for Jonah to go through the streets of Nineveh and proclaim God's message of doom. Read his message in Jonah 3:4. The common people of Nineveh repented first, then the nobles. Think of a city like Chicago repenting and turning to God in one day because of the preaching of a modern prophet. What a miracle! But this is what happened when Jonah preached in his day.

What did Jonah do when Nineveh repented? He sat and sulked on the hill under a plant God "prepared" for shade and pouted. Read what happened (Jon. 4).

The book ends abruptly, but before moving on notice two things in this book. First, Jonah is a type of Christ in His death, burial and resurrection (Matt. 12:40). Second, Jonah is a type of Israel—disobedient to God, swallowed by the nations of the world, who will yet give her up when Christ comes. Then shall Israel be witnesses of God everywhere.

MICAH'S MESSAGE

Micah was a country preacher who lived about 20 miles south of Jerusalem in the town of Morashtite on the Philistine border. He was preaching there to the common people at the same time Isaiah was preaching to people at court in Jerusalem.

Micah prophesied concerning Samaria, the capital of Israel, and Jerusalem, the capital of Judah, but the main part of his prophecy was for Judah. The kings Jotham, Ahaz and Hezekiah reigned in Judah during Micah's day. Oppression was within the walls and foes were coming from without. The condition was the same both in Judah and in Israel.

A Message to the People Micah 1,2

As the book opens we hear the cry, *Hear, O peoples, all of you* (1:2). God was not asleep. He knew the sad condition of His people. Samaria and Jerusalem were guilty before the great Judge of the universe. Captivity and exile were their fate. Micah told them Samaria, the capital of Israel, would fall (1:6,7) and a similar judgment would come upon Judah.

The sins of the people are stated in Micah 2:1-11. God was going to bring suffering and shame upon them for their unscrupulous use of power. He rebuked them for social injustice, unfaithfulness, dishonesty and idolatry. They oppressed the poor and drove women and children from their homes. Micah especially denounced the spread of idolatry and its terrible evils to Judah under King Ahaz. God found their oppression, violence and injustice incurable.

A Message to the Rulers Micah 3—5

In Micah 3:1-4, God likens the rulers' covetousness and self-aggrandizement, even at the price of blood, to cannibalism. The leaders are devouring the poor, defenseless people (3:2,3). The nation was ready to collapse and the princes and priests were responsible. God denounced the sin of the rulers (3:9), the bribery among the judges (3:11), and the false prophets who led the people astray (3:5).

Micah, brokenhearted, tells of God's judgment upon Judah for their sins. Jerusalem and its Temple will be destroyed (3:12) and the people of Judah will be taken captive to Babylon (4:10). But Micah also brings the message of God's love and mercy. God will bring His people back from captivity (4:1–8). Micah was a prophet of hope. He always looked beyond doom and punishment to the day of glory when Christ Himself shall reign, when peace shall cover the earth. God gives the promise. The Messiah will come. Little Bethlehem, smallest among the towns of Judah, shall be honored by the birth of our Lord (5:2-4). When He came as a little babe to bring salvation to a world so in need of a Redeemer, this 700-year-old prophecy from Micah led the wise men to Jerusalem to seek the new King.

God's Argument Micah 6,7

In Micah 6 God is pictured as bringing a lawsuit against His people. He reminded them of how good He had been to them and how He had kept His covenant with them and asked why they had ignored Him. The people, conscience-smitten, asked how they could please God. Frantically they asked if burnt offerings would do (6:6,7). Man is always trying to get back in the good graces of God with some outward religious service or some material goods.

The Old Testament gives us a definition of religion and tells what God requires of you. Read Micah 6:8. How does this compare with man's present-day definitions of "religion"? Do justice—have good ethics in all of life. Love mercy—show consideration for others, when justice has not been done. Walk humbly with thy God—have a personal relationship with God.

It is interesting that when Christ summed up the

175

same matter in Matthew 23:23, He used the words justice, mercy and faithfulness. He thus equated "faithfulness" with "walking humbly with our God," an apt comparison.

More and more we are realizing the social value of the gospel of the Lord Jesus Christ. Wherever this gospel goes conditions are bettered and a brotherhood which is based on sonship is developed. Heart worship of God always issues in practical demonstrations of changed lives.

The Northern Kingdom of Israel did not heed the prophet's warnings and was taken into captivity during Micah's lifetime. Judah did, and was spared for 150 years.

Minimum Daily Requirements/Spiritual Vitamins
Sunday: Doom and deliverance (Obad. 1—21)
Monday: A fish story (Jon. 1,2)
Tuesday: An obedient prophet (Jon. 3,4)
Wednesday: A message to the people (Mic. 1,2)
Thursday: A message to the rulers (Mic. 3,4)
Friday: Birth and rejection of the King (Mic. 5)
Saturday: A message to God's people (Mic. 6,7)

Jesus Christ,
a Stronghold in the Day of Trouble;
the God of My Salvation; a Jealous Lord

Just Before the Doom (Nahum, Habakkuk, Zephaniah)

In name and in message "Nahum" means "comfort." Deliverance for Judah and destruction of Assyria was Nahum's great theme. That Capernaum, where Christ the Comforter performed so many works, means "village of Nahum" (comfort) is noteworthy.

Nahum was probably a native of Galilee and lived at the time of good King Hezekiah and the prophet Isaiah. No doubt, when the Assyrians invaded Israel, he escaped into the Southern Kingdom of Judah. He probably took up his residence in Jerusalem where seven years later he witnessed the siege of that city by Sennacherib which ended with the miraculous destruction of the Assyrian host. Nahum 1:2 may refer to this.

In Nahum 1 we see God the holy Judge of heaven judging the wicked city of Nineveh. The beginning of the vision is awe-inspiring. Read Nahum 1:2. To think of a God like this makes us examine ourselves.

How this thought drives us into the loving arms of a Saviour who is our "covering for sin" and clothes us with the robes of His righteousness.

Notice God did not bring judgment on Assyria in haste. He is *slow to anger*, merciful and gracious, long-suffering and forgiving, yet He will by no means clear the guilty (1:3).

Nahum 1:8-14 states the battle-and-destruction sentence upon corrupt Nineveh. She has been weighed in the balance and found wanting. The picture of the siege and fall of Nineveh and the desolation which followed are described with graphic eloquence. God would make an end of her with an overrunning flood (2:6), her name would be utterly cut off and He would dig her grave (1:14). The mustering of the armies around Nineveh, and the marshaling of the forces within the city are pictured in such a way that the prophet makes his hearers see all the horrid sights of the tragic scene.

The Medes and Babylonians completely destroyed Nineveh in 607 B.C. It occurred at the zenith of her power. According to Nahum's prophecy, it came true that a sudden rise of the Tigris, carried away a great part of the wall and assisted the attacking army of the Medes and Babylonians in its overthrow. Nineveh was also partly destroyed by fire (3:13,15).

Nineveh is a type of all nations that turn their backs on God. In our day, proud civilizations are staking everything upon the strength of manpower and machines, and there is a terrible disregard of God. We find that Nineveh was overthrown because of her sin (3:1-7) and that her great wealth and strength were not sufficient to save her (3:8-19). Nations often depend upon might and power to survive. They forget that the person or nation that deliberately and finally rejects God, deliberately and finally and fatally elects doom. Beware of this!

HABAKKUK'S QUESTION

Habakkuk was a prophet (Hab. 1:1), and he was one of the Levitical choristers in the Temple (3:19) and helped in the arranging of the services. We know little about this prophet except that he asked questions and received answers. He, like many men today, could not reconcile his belief in a good and righteous God with the facts of life as he saw them. He was troubled with an eternal "Why?" Even today a man of faith finds himself bewildered at many things that are going on round about him. We ask, "Why does God allow such awful crimes to go unchecked if He is all-powerful?"

This book seems to be a dialogue between Jehovah and the prophet. Two conversations are recorded and the book closes with a hymn which reveals a new confidence in God.

The Dialogue Habakkuk 1,2

Habakkuk was confused and bewildered. It seemed to him that God was doing nothing to straighten out the conditions in the world. The prophet had lived during the great reformation under King Josiah. Assyria had fallen just as Nahum had prophesied. Egypt and Babylon had then contended for the place of power. At the battle of Carchemish, 605 B.C., the Babylonians were conquerors and the Babylonians and Chaldeans were united under Nebuchadnezzar.

Habakkuk knew only too well that Judah must fall before this great rising power. The world about him was in an upheaval and it seemed that God was doing nothing about it.

But worse, he saw his own land, Judah, full of lawlessness and tyranny. The righteous were oppressed (1:4,13). The people were living in open sin. They were worshiping idols (2:18,19). They were oppressing the poor. Habakkuk knew that the day was dark. He knew that this sin was leading to an invasion of Jerusalem by a strong enemy. But one question arose in his mind and troubled him greatly. Why should any nation as wicked as Babylon conquer a nation like Judah which was less evil?

Habakkuk asked God his questions. Read what God answered in Habakkuk 1:5-11. God told Habakkuk that He was not indifferent to His people. He was already working. The Chaldeans were to punish Judah. They were a cruel scourge which would sweep over the land to destroy it.

God's answer horrified Habakkuk. He could not understand how God would allow such awful means to bring about the punishing of His people, Judah. How could He use such a cruel scourge? How was it possible for God to use such an enemy to punish His own people when He Himself is so pure and holy? Listen to Habakkuk challenge God in Habakkuk 1:13 to defend His actions.

Habakkuk expected God to answer him, so he climbed up on the watchtower to wait (2:1). Read God's answer in Habakkuk 2:2-20. God admitted the wickedness of the Chaldeans but declared that they would destroy themselves by their own evil. Pride and cruelty always bring destruction. It may have seemed that the Chaldeans were prospering, but they were doomed. Habakkuk 2:4 summarizes this idea and is the heart of the book.

Habakkuk's Song Habakkuk 3

Read Habakkuk's prayer in chapter 3. Habakkuk is the prophet who sang in the night. Read the magnificent melody with which the prophecy closes in Habakkuk 3:17,18.

Habakkuk realized that God was in control of this universe and that He was working out His own purpose in His own time. Habakkuk learned that he could trust implicitly in God. He realized that he could see only a small part of God's plan at one time. One must wait for God to reveal His entire program and believe God's way is best. God does not promise that He will unravel every problem, but we can put our trust in Him (read Ps. 37:5 and 2 Tim. 1:12).

ZEPHANIAH AND THE COMING JUDGMENT

Little is known of Zephaniah. His name means "hidden of Jehovah." Very likely he was a prince of the royal house of Judah, being a descendant of Hezekiah. Thus he was in a position to denounce the sins of the princes since he himself was an aristocrat.

Zephaniah began his ministry as a prophet in the early days of the reign of Josiah (641-610 B.C.) who undertook to promote a religious revival. Two wicked and idol-worshiping kings had preceded Josiah and the land was overrun with social injustice and moral corruption.

Zephaniah said Jehovah was in the midst of the

land for judgment (Zeph. 1). He first searches Judah and condemns the idol worshipers (vv. 4,5), those who swear by God one time and at another time by other gods (v. 5) and those who turned back from the Lord (v. 6). The land had to be freed from idolatry. The prophet called the people to seek God (2:1-3), and he declared that nothing could save the nation from God's anger but real repentance.

Then he turned to the five heathen nations of Philistia, Moab, Ammon, Ethiopia and Assyria. They, too, would be visited with the wrath of God because of their pride and scorn toward the Lord's people (2:10). Notice how the desolation of Nineveh is described in wonderfully accurate terms in Zephaniah 2:13-15. The judgment on Israel's local enemies (2:4-15) was literally fulfilled. The judgment on Israel's enemies over this wide world is yet to be fulfilled. Read God's Word in Zephaniah 3:8 and then 2:10,11.

God also says the idols of their enemies shall be destroyed, and that everyone shall worship God in his own country (2:11). Instead of all having to make a pilgrimage to Jerusalem, they may worship God anywhere. The Jews taught that Jerusalem was the place of worship, but Zephaniah taught that spiritual worship did not depend upon a place but on the Presence of God.

The prophet concluded with wonderful promises of Israel's future restoration and of the happy state of the purified people of God in the latter days (Zeph. 3). The redeemed remnant will return cleansed, humbled, trusting and rejoicing with their offerings to Zion. They will be established in their land with God "in their midst" (3:15,17).

182

The rejoicing of Zephaniah 3:14-20 must refer to something beside the day when the remnant will return after the captivity of Babylon. Judah's worst judgment followed that return. She has seen little but misery ever since. Neither did anything like this occur at Christ's first coming. It must refer to the day when the Lord Himself shall sit on the throne of David, when His people shall be gathered from the four corners of the earth. This prophecy shall be fulfilled when Christ comes to reign in power and great glory.

Minimum Daily Requirements/Spiritual Vitamins
Sunday: The judge and the verdict (Nah. 1)
Monday: The execution (Nah. 2,3)
Tuesday: Habakkuk's complaint (Hab. 1)
Wednesday: God's reply (Hab. 2)
Thursday: Habakkuk's song (Hab. 3)
Friday: Coming judgments (Zeph. 1,2)
Saturday: The kingdom blessings (Zeph. 3)

Jesus Christ,
the Desire of All Nations;
the Righteous Branch;
the Sun of Righteousness

Encouragement from God (Haggai, Zechariah, Malachi)

Haggai, Zechariah and Malachi are the last of the prophetic books. Each of these prophets prophesied to the Jews after they returned to Jerusalem. Remember that Nebuchadnezzar captured Jerusalem and completely destroyed the Temple. In Ezra we found that when Cyrus, king of Persia, issued a decree permitting all the captives to return to Jerusalem and to rebuild their Temple, only about 50,000 returned.

Haggai is the first voice to be heard after the exile. His name means "my feast." His book is a collection of four brief messages written between August and December in the second year of Darius, 520 B.C.

HAGGAI'S MESSAGES

The handful of Jews who returned to Jerusalem under Zerubbabel and began to build the Temple were few in number, poor, harassed by enemies and worse, they had lost the inner strength that comes from a joy in the Lord. Because of all this the work dragged. The people lost heart and became selfish and they made no progress beyond laying the Temple foundation. They became more interested in building homes for themselves than for God (Hag. 1:4).

God would not allow this to go on, so He sent punishment as a result. Poor crops, droughts, scanty trade, misery and turmoil made their spirits fail. They were working and slaving but finding no real joy.

It was then that Haggai gave his first message (1:1-11). His stern call proved to be a good tonic. Zerubbabel (the governor of Jerusalem), Joshua (the high priest) and the people began again the work of rebuilding the Temple.

Note how long after the first message the second one (2:1-9) was given (1:1; 2:1). For the history of this period read Ezra 3:8-13.

As the people were building, a new discouragement seized them. Those who remembered the splendor of the Temple of Solomon were greatly disappointed in this new Temple. How inferior in size and costliness the stones were! How much smaller in extent the foundation was! And besides, this second Temple would not have the things that made the first one so glorious—the Ark, the Shekinah, and all that went with the service of the high priest. These pessimists dampened the enthusiasm of the builders.

But Haggai came with a word of cheer. God was going to pour His resources into that new building (Hag. 2:7,9). What a comfort this must have been!

The third message (2:10-19) of cleansing and blessing was delivered three months after the Temple was started. By the use of questions and answers Haggai showed the people their impurity. He made them realize their sinfulness. He showed them the reason their prayers were not answered was because they had put off so long the completing of the Temple. They had spoiled all that they had done because of their guilt. If they would renew their zeal, they would find God would bless them.

The Book of Haggai closes with a final message of hope (2:20-23). God tells of the end of national governments and the establishing of His kingdom. Read the promise to Zerubbabel in Haggai 2:23.

ZECHARIAH AND THE MESSIAH

Zechariah was the prophet of restoration and glory. Born in Babylon, he was priest as well as prophet. Zechariah, whose name meant "Jehovah remembers," prophesied for three years. The glorious future, rather than the sad present, was his message. He was a poet, while Haggai was a plain, practical preacher.

In Zechariah chapter 1 we find Judah still a remnant, Jerusalem far from restored and the Gentile nations at ease round about her. Zechariah, a young prophet who had stood alongside the aged Haggai, strengthened the children of Israel as they built the Temple and warned them not to disappoint God as their fathers had done. He pictured God's love and care for His people. He quickened their hopes by painting in glowing colors the time of perpetual blessing that was coming to Israel in the far off ages.

Zechariah does not condemn the people but tells of the presence of God to strengthen and help. He especially encourages the governor, Zerubbabel, who was conscious of his own weakness. Hear what Zechariah says, *Not by might nor by power, but by My Spirit, says the Lord of hosts* (4:6).

The Messiah and the Kingdom

Zechariah foretells the Saviour more than any other prophet except Isaiah.

Christ the Branch (3:8)

Christ my Servant (3:8)

Christ's entry into Jerusalem on a colt (9:9)

Christ, the good Shepherd (9:16; 11:11)

Christ betrayed for 30 pieces of silver (11:12,13)

Christ pierced (12:10)

Christ's people saved (12:10; 13:1)

Christ, the smitten Shepherd (13:7)

Christ's coming on Mount of Olives (14:3-8)

Zechariah chapters 9—14 are full of promises of the coming Messiah and a worldwide kingdom. The prophet does not picture a city rebuilt on its old foundations, but a glorious city whose wall is the Lord. It is not armed for war but is filled with peace because the Prince of Peace reigns. He shall come the first time as the lowly One, riding upon a humble beast (9:9). But we see this lowly One becoming a mighty Sovereign (14:8-11). The Messiah in all His glory and might shall put all the enemies under His feet and He shall establish His kingdom in Jerusalem and sit upon the throne of David (9:10).

If one follows these chapters closely, he discovers victory over all the enemies of Israel. Chapter 11 reveals the Shepherd who would seek to save Israel but be rejected. He will be sold for 30 pieces of silver, the price of a slave. This foreshadowed Christ and His betrayal by Judas. Chapter 12 gives us the prophecy of the siege of Jerusalem by the Antichrist and his armies in the last days. Then we see the repentance of the Jews (12:12) when they shall see

Him whom they have pierced. The fountain shall be opened to the house of David for sin and uncleanness (13:1). Then we see the return of the Messiah upon the Mount of Olives, which will be split in half (14:4). He left the earth at that same spot with the promise of His return (see Acts 1:11). Finally He shall be King over the whole earth and all people shall be holy unto Him (Zech. 14:9-20).

MALACHI, THE LAST PROPHET

We have now come to the last book in the Old Testament. By this time, a hundred years or more had passed since the Jews had returned to Jerusalem after the captivity in Babylon. Malachi is the last prophet to speak to Israel in her own land. (Israel here means all the remnant of Israel and Judah that returned after the exile.)

The first enthusiasm after the return from Babylon had passed. The skeptical attitude among the people showed itself in religious coldness and social laxity. This is always true. The priests had become irreverent and neglectful (Mal. 1:6,11,12). The prophet rebukes the careless priests for offering in sacrifice to God worthless animals that they would not offer to the governor. They had lost sight of their high calling and deserved the ignominy heaped upon them. They refused to work except for money. God's condemnation began with the leaders (2:1-9) because as long as the priests were openly unfit, what could be expected from the people at large?

What would you think of a person who held something before his eyes and then complained that he couldn't see anything? What would you suggest to solve the difficulty? This is just what Malachi had to do. The Jews could not see that God's love had been of any special advantage to them because sin was blocking their vision.

The carelessness of the leaders had resulted in a carelessness among God's people in keeping themselves separate from the heathen nations. Mixed marriages with women outside the tribes became common. Some men had not hesitated to divorce their Jewish wives to make this possible (2:10-16). Another result of this laxity of loyalty to God was in the growing prevalence of social sin (3:5). Malachi 3:7 reveals the religious indifference and skepticism of the people. The Jews had been cured of idolatry, but they had grown careless and indifferent about many things. They had neglected the house of God. They had robbed God of their tithes and offerings.

This attitude of the people was probably due to the feelings that the glowing promises of Haggai and Zechariah and of the other prophets had not been realized. They said that Jehovah did not seem to distinguish between good and bad men (2:17). He blessed all alike, and evil men often flourished at the expense of their fellows. What's the use of being good? Is this not one of the standing complaints of those who think they are good men? They say, "What is God doing that He permits such things?"

The answer to such a complaint is that God does care. He showed this to them by saying that one day He will send His messenger to prepare His way. Then He will come in person "suddenly" and sit in judgment and separate the evil from the good (3:1). His judgment will be searching and effective (3:2,3).

189

When God really gets ready to act, the action will be final.

Read Malachi 1:2 again. *"I have loved you,"* says *the Lord.* What a message to a people who had sinned as Israel had and had spurned the love of God. God wants all His children to honor and adore Him. He longs to have us obey and worship Him. God is unchanging. He never forgets His promises of undying love and everlasting mercy.

Minimum Daily Requirements/Spiritual Vitamins
Sunday: Haggai's message (Hag. 1,2)
Monday: Visions (Zech. 1—6)
Tuesday: Fasts (Zech. 7,8)
Wednesday: Restoration (Zech. 9—11)
Thursday: The Messiah (Zech. 12—14)
Friday: Sins of priests and people (Mal. 1,2)
Saturday: Message of hope (Mal. 3,4)

400 Years of Silence

From Nehemiah to the beginning of New Testament times, 400 years elapsed. During this period no biblical prophet spoke or wrote. In fact, it is called the "period of silence." It is important to know some of the things that happened between the days of Nehemiah and Malachi and the birth of Christ.

Before he died, Alexander the Great divided his empire among his four generals because he had no heirs to his throne. Egypt and later Palestine went to his general Ptolemy. Great numbers of Jews at this time settled in Egypt and other centers of culture, spreading everywhere the knowledge of their God and their hope of a Messiah.

During this time, about 285 B.C., the Old Testament was translated into Greek. This version of the Scriptures is called the "Septuagint," meaning 70, because 70 noted Hebrew scholars did the work.

Then the Syrian kingdom arose. In the conflicts between Syria and Egypt, Antiochus Epiphanes, king of Syria, seized Palestine. The Jews were forbidden by Antiochus Epiphanes to worship in the Temple and were compelled to eat the flesh of swine, which God through Moses had forbidden (Lev. 11:1-8). Many Jews refused and a period of martyrdom began.

The cruelties of Antiochus Epiphanes brought about the revolt of the Maccabees. Aroused by the patriotism and religious ardor of Mattathias, a group of patriotic Jews gathered about him and began an insurrection that spread rapidly. When he died, his son Judas took his place. In an attempt to crush this rebellion under the Maccabees, Antiochus was defeated in three deadly conflicts. The band of ragged but loyal Jews, inspired by an undying faith in God, came out victorious!

In 63 B.C., Rome gained possession of Palestine, preparing the way and the time for Jesus to be born. The Jews had some political liberty, but were required to pay a yearly tax to the Roman government. From here, the story is continued in the New Testament.